The Ripple Effect

Countdown to Freedom

To P. J.

Normand Desmarais

authorHOUSE®

AuthorHouse™
1663 Liberty Drive
Bloomington, IN 47403
www.authorhouse.com
Phone: 1-800-839-8640

First published by AuthorHouse 10/29/2010

ISBN: 978-1-4520-9160-0 (hc)
ISBN: 978-1-4520-9161-7 (sc)
ISBN: 978-1-4520-9162-4 (e)

Library of Congress Control Number: 2010915077

Printed in the United States of America

This book is printed on acid-free paper.

Acknowledgements:

I WOULD LIKE TO ACKNOWLEDGE my sister Rita and brother Raymond for our life long friendship and the years of morally supporting each other. My sister Rita for keeping me calm collected and focused on the project at hand. I want to thank my brother Raymond for giving us this phrase "The world would be a better place when;" "The Power of Love replaces the Love of Power." Lastly I wish to thank my dear friend Marie for being proud of what I am doing. I truly appreciate their support.

This Book is dedicated to all who are needlessly suffering and to those who have already needlessly suffered and died.

Preface:

I MAY BE AN UNKNOWN nobody, but I am an angry unknown nobody who seeks to spread the words of those who care. One of those that wants the rest of the world to know of the injustices and lies forced on innocent people on a daily basis. I am only repeating what I have learned, but I am sending it out in my own words. It is my understanding that we all see and hear things differently, so if the same information is sent out in many different ways that many more would understand and be enlightened. Those people would then let others know until finally the whole world will change for the betterment of all.

It would be very wrong of me to know what I know and to not share my knowledge. I would be just as guilty as the villains who kill and maim for profit. There are many subjects covered in this booklet. The articles may have been written in slightly different formats, this is not intentional, this is the way I write. These are my thoughts….my opinions.

I believe in free speech and intend to do so. I realize that many will disagree, that is their choice. I suspect that those in their present beneficial positions, will be very angry with me and others. They will fight very hard to prevent being exposed for the greedy uncaring individuals that they are.

"Observations of a raving lunatic" is the title I would receive from those in positions of power or so called authority. They would place this title on me for fear of loosing what they have, if the truth were known about them. Even those too far up the back end of those in authority, are blinded from the truth and reality for they would lose their cushy positions and pay as well.

So many good intentioned people have been bribed, have been threatened with life and limb, or have completely disappeared simply because they attempted to warn us of the corruption that entraps us, often without our knowledge. We have been living a lie for well over 2000 years. This illusion has been continuous to us through lies and falsehoods, feeding on our ignorance (not knowing the facts). Through time it has been refined and polished to what we have today.

These people who run and ruin our lives have the incredible ability to sweet talk, to twist the truth, and camouflage the facts from the public, in order to keep their positions of power and authority. Why is that? Simple they have no other honest way to survive in our society, except to leech off those that are value producers (those that actually work for a living). Not hard to do after over 2000 years of practice in the perfection of double talk.

The North American First Nation People have a name for this. "Forked Tongue" a title that fits perfectly. These are people who can smile at you, give you a warm friendly handshake and a promise, while stabbing you in the back and at the same time pull the rug from under you. They are wolves camouflaged as good, honest, caring people.

Now the decision is…should the attempt at informing the public be "subdued" or "no holds barred"? Tell it like I see it, no beating around the bush. Yes I know that's a cliché, but I'll use them if it helps to better explain what I want to say.

Should love and compassion be used? Applying completely honest intentions, shinning the light of truth into the darkness of deceit and lies? Throwing light over the twisted truths and deceptions employed to retract more and more power and freedoms from us, to subjugate us into a nation of servitude and compliance.

Our education system has been compromised since the beginning of the 1900's, further restricting our inherent need to create some sort of positive, happy productive future. At least that's what they want you to believe, to be happy safe and healthy, and yet we are on the whole, miserable, insulted and unhealthy.

This book attempts to explain why.

This manuscript covers a variety of subjects. Each on their own could be its own book. My attempt here is to show you that upon closer inspection that they are connected in many ways. How they help and compliment each other to achieve their individual ends. By this I mean if you look at one at a time it may not appear to be all that harmful to you. But when they all work together that is where their real power lays. Open your minds and start paying attention to the man behind the curtain. Do not lay back and let it happen.

Contents

Chapter One: Pharmaceuticals

Feb 2010

2:20 P.M. SATURDAY AFTERNOON WAS finally here and James stopped his car at the curb in front of Ronnie's place, his host and best friend, for this beautiful sunny afternoon. The temperature was just perfect for a day of swimming and barbequing. The day promised to be enjoyable, socializing with his other friends who should arrive shortly.

As James got out of his car his other friend Martin and his wife Shelly drove up in the old Chevy with the fish symbol on its trunk lid, for Martin was the religious one of the group. As Martin shut the car engine off it sputtered and coughed. "Hey, Martin" yelled James, "give your car a tune-up and that won't happen any more". To which Martin retorted "God will take care of it, I have faith".

They both walked along the side of Ronnie's place and saw him talking to Richie and Hank who were sitting at the table under a fully grown Maple tree. Malcolm and Jeff were all ready in the pool with Malcolm's wife and their two children. Ronny turned and saw them saying "well were all here, lets all have a drink to celebrate our first get together of the summer".

Ronny was the most read and educated of this whole group, and also the wealthiest, but was very down to earth. All his friends gathered here today respected him very much. Ronny did not flaunt his wealth or knowledge and often helped with advise or funds without asking for anything in return. He himself nor did any of the friends have any idea that this beautiful day would be the beginning of something that would change their lives.

Ronnie's life mate Catherine followed by Jen, Jeff's girlfriend stepped out the sliding door and onto the deck. Both were carrying large plates full of snacks, and Catherine called out, "hey every one, here are some snacks to munch on till we start the barbeque". Ronny ran up on to the deck to help, and when finished he in turn and yelled for all to hear, "bars open".

The bar was well stocked with both spirits and assorted beers, for Ronny knew that his friends did not all have the same tastes. As James approached the bar he nodded to Ronny saying, "Your house is not only spacious and gorgeous your bar is also a livable space, I like it". "Thank you very much, James,"' replied Ronny. "What's your poison?" "I'll have a scotch on the rocks," James replied. this time the others were at the bar placing their orders. Soon the small talk started and the day moved on quite nicely.

"Well, That was one heck of a meal Catherine", Malcolm exclaimed after emitting a loud audible belch and then with a smile excused himself as he pulled his hand from his mouth. Catherine smiled and said, "thank you, I can tell you enjoyed it", as she placed the last dish on the tray to return to the house. Grace leaned over and reprimanded him for such an ignorant display.

Grace was Malcolm's wife for fifteen years whose two children were also obese. Grace and her family were well aware of this and felt uncomfortable in public. Yet they felt accepted at Ronnie's place. They had both agreed that one day they would try and find a way to loose weight.

Ronny and Catherine we're the couple with perfect health, minds and money. They were both aware of the problems of their guests and had decided to help them in any way they could. Their patience was to finally pay off this day.

Just then James stepped onto the deck saying "I'm glad the washroom is not too far away from here". He had a prostate problem that all were aware of but said nothing for fear of insulting James. He had already decided to ask Ronny and Catherine how and why they looked so healthy.

As James sat down and grabbed his drink he shocked every one by asking, "Ronny why are you two the picture of health and the rest of us look like we do?" "Funny you should ask that James", replied Ronny. "Catherine and I have been searching for a way to help all of you, but we were waiting for the right time".

Just then Catherine interrupted by saying, "maybe now is the time". The group smiled for they had been thinking the same thing. Sensing this Ronny asked the group "would you all be willing to seek my advice?" They all nodded in agreement.

"Let us start with James since he is the one who mentioned it first Ok?" They all agreed. "Well, let me start by telling you a few little stories that I have heard".

Just last week he had an operation on his leg to correct a blood circulation problem. Now he is complaining about it being cold and uncomfortable, and he can barely move it. His daughter felt the cold leg and asked, "whats wrong now? Are you going to have to go in again?" Two days later, after having more tests done Mr. Blake was told that his foot would have to be removed just above the ankle. Since blood congealed for some unknown reasons in the foot, greatly slowing down the return flow up his leg to the heart.

Mr. Blake wondered to himself, "how did I get to become diabetic and why is there no cure? Sometimes I think my life is just not worth living, not this way. Not with all this pain and useless medications that do not seem to help".

Mr. Blake's daughter Cathy spends her day wondering why both her parents, good honest working people should be afflicted each with a different set of health problems. Cathy's mother is very close to death at this time due to kidney failure. Cathy is now at the stage of fear at hearing the phone ring, the fear of the final call of her mother has passed.

She wonders why with all the advancements in medicine should this be happening, and decides that life is just not only unfair but cruel. What illness is she in for? What of her husband? She glances at her son sitting on the couch playing a video game. What fate is in store for him? How can I save him when I am helplessly watching my parents suffer and die? Glancing at the clock she rushes off to work.

"That's amazing", announced James, "You heard these and they are real" "Yes" replied Ronny, "and here is a hypothetical story based on what I have heard from several groups in the know". "Tell us", pleaded Grace, loving a good story. The rest of them leaned forward not wanting to miss a word. Ronny started.

On a bright sunny day at the private exclusive golf club in Florida, George is at the tee. He looks down at the ball then down the fairway and remarks to Bill chief CEO of one the most powerful government bodies in the country, "Life is great. My company earned over $40,000,000.00 in profit in just the first quarter of this year. I just love my drug company". Bill replied with a smile, "you just don't care how many people suffer buying the bogus crap you call drugs do you?". "How else can I afford to give you your large bonus every year?" George remarked.

"Apparently you were born without much of a conscience were you?" asked Bill as he scanned the green two hundred and fifty yards away. "I, like you have decided that it has a way of getting in the way of profits. Anyway I don't care how many people suffer and die as long as we make hefty sales", George looked at the ball, and with great concentration raised his arms then took his swing. He cursed out loud as the ball fell short of the green.

Several hours later after the golf game George stood in the boardroom staring out the plate glass window down at the sprawling city far below. He thought to himself, "how can we get more profits from those stupid idiots down there?" Just then many of the top company executives entered the large room. They sat in their own comfortable and expensive chairs.

As George turned around and started walking to the head of the table he noticed one of his staff was already seated and with a grin from ear to ear. "What's with you, today Stan? You look like you won the lottery again". "Sir you won't believe it but I have come up with a solution to the question you posed to us last week. I can just see my bonus pay now".

"Well don't sit there like an idiot! Tell me". "Well, sir, it's like this. We start a pandemic". "I like it already" George interrupted then said "continue". "We start a pandemic then advertise how deadly it is and cause mass hysteria. We then develop a new drug which we sell at a huge profit to combat this new threat. Then we get the government to back us into forcing the people to be inoculated.

The sweet part is the government pays for it all. We will make a killing on it in more ways then one, since a large number of people will die, causing the majority to fall in and voluntarily take the drug. We can't loose". "That's fantastic", George interjected, "what do the rest of you think?" With one hundred percent of the yes vote they started planning.

George asked Stan, "How are you enjoying your bonus?" "Yes" Stan replied. "I bought a villa on the west coast of Greece and a seventy- five foot yacht to cruise the Mediterranean Sea". "Good for you" George remarked, "I see your spending it wisely. Tell me, how is the pandemic doing?" "Well" Stan said, with a very large grin, "we raked in sixty four million in the first month and we're well on our way to doubling that this month.

We also calculated that this pandemic will run its course for another ten months". George turned around looked out the penthouse office window, mentally calculating huge profits. Combining drug sales and this pandemic he figured roughly four point four billion in generated revenues for just one year. Ah life is wonderful he thought.

"You can't get a sweeter deal then this. With government backing we have the new born getting their first needle and the profits start from there. I only wish I had gotten into the food industry as well. Those bastards are making a killing. Well, you've got to share the wealth I suppose".

At that moment, Stan announced that the profits they were making having their scientists come up with addictive formulas for the food industry were in excess of millions per month. George turned in surprise. "What did you say?" Stan repeated and added "Mr. Brooks got us involved in that two years before you came on board". George replied, "smart man that Mr. Brooks".

As he walked out the door, Stan stopped and slowly turned around, "should we not be a little concerned of the amount of deaths?" George looked up at Stan with amazement in his eyes, "are you kidding me? It don't matter how many we kill. There are plenty of them out there. And anyway they breed like rabbits, so we'll never run out of those stupid money making fools. They are a constantly producing profit machine. So don't worry. Go sail your yacht and keep a smile on your face". Stan thanked George, and with a smile on his face walked out of the office

"Is this true?" asked Richie in amazement. "Yes" replied Ronny "the concept is, but the names are changed to protect the guilty. These types of people do exist and actually do these things I just mentioned". "That's all well and good for you to talk about, but what has that got to do with helping us" asked Malcolm.

"Well first of all, you need to know some of the causes that effect us in our daily lives in regards to Wealth, Health and happiness" replied Ronny. "Each one of you in this group is afflicted with one or more problems that is caused by the medical, government, and religious groups. All of your problems can and will be solved if you listen and follow up on what you hear from myself and Catherine".

"There is room on this world for every one to be healthy and well off.

Let us start with James. He and his family suffer from many medical problems

Martin is very religious and is very confused and starting to feel very frustrated and is unsure as to why. Richie thinks the government is out to get him but since he can't put his finger on the cause, he too is frustrated.

"Hank is always down and out, and has been divorced twice. He can't seem to get his head above the water line. Malcolm and his family are uncomfortable with their obesity. Then there is Jeff who is not aware of the meaning of what history tries to tell us and why it keeps on repeating".

"Well, all of us can benefit from the many stories and knowledge that Catherine and I have, and would love to share with you". A warm gentle breeze wafted over Catherine's long, beautiful red hair as she stood and announced, "would any one like a snack?" Richie said "hope it won't take too long I want to hear more of what Ronny has to say". Grace quickly got up to help Catherine with getting the snacks.

As every one was again seated Ronny continued. "We the many live our lives under the rules of a chosen few. They are the chosen few because they have placed themselves in those positions. That way we do the hard work and they live the easy life". "Why?" asked Jeff. "Well it's simple, really. They are too lazy to do any real work of a productive value. At the same time they make us feel as if we are the guilty ones, and that they must tell us what to do, think, and say.

"They want to keep the power and prestige that they have worked so hard for in conniving and lies. They will do what it takes to keep this control. This is why they try to find more and more ways to take as much money from us as they can. It is easier to rule over a poor and unhealthy population. I will explain more as we go along okay?" They all nodded.

Ronny stood up and motioned for them to listen and said let me tell you another story.

Right from birth we are given our first needle, one that most of us do not really need, since most mothers try to take the best precautions they possibly can. They want to be proud of giving birth to a beautiful healthy, baby. Most do not smoke or drink alcohol or abuse themselves while pregnant. They try to stay healthy and eat the best possible foods to ensure the health of their child to be.

It is an inherent desire in most women to deliver the world's perfect healthy baby.

A parent wants a child who will contribute to society in a positive manner as well as having a long happy productive life. A parent wants a child they can be proud of. This is a basic human need.

Meanwhile we do not realize that the foods we eat are filled with toxins, poisons and drugs, to harm us and keep us addicted to them; keeping us coming back for more. Go to a plaza and find a seat to sit on and observe the people walking by. You will notice a larger amount of overweight and unhealthy people over fairly healthy looking ones.

Why is that? Well for one thing improper eating habits and exercise brought on by advertising and chemically induced foods are to blame. We are treated like pigs at the trough being fed trash and scraps of worthless value, yet we gullibly consume what we are handed. We are unknowingly self inflicting our own ill health and paying the food and drug companies to destroy our bodies for their own profits.

Even the water we drink is poisoned by chlorine known to destroy brain cells, thus reducing the efficiency of the brain. This in turn helps in turning the population into a mindless working force that is easier to control. We are brainwashed into believing that prescription drugs are the only thing that can make us healthier.

We are told that our body is unable to heal itself without drugs. So we gladly buy this drug for that, and this drug for that. Have you ever heard two people talking about how I am using this drug for my blood pressure and this drug to keep my blood thinner? Yet I still have this persistent bloating or something or other? I also have to take the medication for the rest of my life. I used to dream about taking a nice vacation but now I can not afford to.

Anyway I am not healthy enough to take one. Most people are blissfully unaware that they are self inflicting their own ill health because the real truth is kept hidden from them. The truth being hidden from us is the proper healthy use of natural herbs and homeopathic medications. Why? It is simply put that the drug companies would loose too much profit. That is all they care about if the truth were told.

Somewhere it has been stated that we now have more diseases and ailments then we did say fifty years ago. Most are made up through the poisons we consume in our foods. Others arrived through the stresses placed upon us through survival in this economy, while others are through many electronic devises placed too close to our bodies, such as cellular phones, pagers and laptops.

The air we inhale is contaminated by all the fossil fuels we burn is another contributing factor. The oil companies, drug companies are in bed with the top government officials in their lust to rule and rob have made it this way. But no, they can not let you know that they did it all, or they would lose control over us, and their profits. We are told to keep the status quo, don't rock, the boat. You can't change it anyway, so don't try. And we obey like nice the little boys and girls that we are. Sort of reminds you of sheep, does it not.

As we blindly watch the mind numbing box we call television we are bombarded with commercials. Forcing upon us all types of commercials telling us, we absolutely need this item or toy, stripping us of our money and prestige. However the worst type of commercial we are inflicted with are the medical ones telling us only their pills and medications will heal us.

With enough repetition you start to believe that your own body is incapable to heal itself, which is a big lie. Cut your finger then watch it bleed a little bit. Wash it with water, then put a bandage on it and wait. Voila. What happened? It's healed, how can this be? My own body healed itself with out pills, medicines or even a doctor. The commercials even have the audacity to tell you that only your doctor knows your body better than you. The unfortunate thing here is that so many people fall for this scam.

The doctors are taught in schools funded by the drug companies. They are trained in anatomy which is good for us, but are sadly trained in the use of handing out useless prescriptions, thus negating any real good that the doctors do for us. Most doctors honestly want to be good at what they are trained for. They, themselves, do not see the harm they are doing in handing out the medications.

Some are just greedy since they know that the more prescriptions they hand out the more they make. Most of the real medicines to assist in healing are not taught to these dedicated people because the medical industry would lose too much in the way of profits. The medical industry is hard at work persuading the government that the growing and usage of natural organic medications should be against the law, with very stiff fines on any person caught growing, selling and using these natural medicines.

Why is it that we sit there watching commercials advertising any type of medicine explaining its benefits for a single physical problem, which we did not even knew existed prior to this revelation, and still we sit there listening to the side effects? Yet people still, like sheep, go and buy this one wonder drug knowing it will cause side effects.

When will they put two and two together and realize it's all about the money? They do not realize this wonder drug will cause other medical problems that will have to be corrected by another wonder drug and so on and so on. When will it sink in that you are being conned, that you are buying your own medical problems.

Through the use of commercials we are also brainwashed into believing that chemotherapy and radiation treatments are the only real cure. Both destroy the immune system or badly damage it. The false cure rate for these money generating treatments are only three percent at most. Women are induced to take a mammogram, and the only real reason for this is to get another customer.

No mammogram has ever saved a woman's life. It is, in reality, a major cause of cancer by squeezing the breast so hard that causes any malignant cyst or node to burst inside the breast. That, in time, will lead to cancer. This is great for the medical field but bad for the woman. The same scenario applies to men as well in regards to say, prostrate inspections. This is just another money grabbing technique.

The real effect that chemotherapy has on the body in regards to the immune system is that it destroys or seriously impairs the immune system. No they can not really tell you since there would be lost revenue to the medical field. I do not mean the real doctors who are honestly trying to help but the top brass whose only motive is the bottom line financially. Every possible means is being utilized to keep us on the brink of near death to suck as much cash as possible. That's damn near total rule with a great cash reward, can't beat that system, no sir.

The big brother factor is here now and the majority of people do not realize it. We are given poisoned food and water, harmful medicines that do not heal, only ease the pain or affliction caused by other induced poisons. The masters have been hard at work creating a population of zombies whose only choice in life is to obey. They have been hard at work on this for the past three thousand years.

For the past one hundred and fifty years their work has been getting somewhat easier. The use of modern discoveries in medicines and chemicals, as well as the electronic age has further assisted in this evil program of control. If we do not soon wake up, realizing what is happening to us and why. It will be too late for us all and we will find ourselves prisoners in a system we blindly built to imprison us.

We see so many movies made on this subject of population control and brainwashing not realizing that the movie makers are trying to warn us. But we still do not seem to grasp the reality that is cleverly being concealed from our drug induced minds. Meanwhile those self appointed demigods laugh at us and realize how easy it is for them to plan and implement their evil goals.

Why? Because as uninformed or blindly following the ruling class we are but individuals with no real power or purpose in life other then to be controlled. which, is what we are led to believe. This is absolutely false; we do have the power to change, simply by saying no, this will not continue. Say to yourself I am free and you cannot control me.

It is a very sad thing when one hears of a doctor or a natural health practitioner that is jailed for saving one or several peoples lives. Without using prescription drugs, these peoples lives are saved and the one's who helped are jailed. Why is it against the law to save a persons life without prescription medication? Well, for one most important thing, no profits were made and also the lost revenue to keep these people alive to use more drugs has now been lost.

Someone must pay for this atrocity. These good doctors are jailed to tell all the other doctors to stay in line and do as they are told or the same will happen to them as well. Fear is a good persuader.

They cannot let the masses know that most if not all diseases are curable and preventable. The economy would suffer and we cannot have that. So who cares how many people needlessly suffer and perish as long as a fortune is made for those immoral sub-humans, as long as the economy is fine and they make the profits. There is no remorse here for the profit makers, just more money to be had.

To appease the stock holders they must come up with new drugs for invented ailments and afflictions that we, the people never even thought we had. Now we are told we have this problem or that affliction so we go out and buy this new miracle cure at an out of this world price, bragging to our neighbors and co-workers that we are taking this or that and how well we are taking care of our health. What stupid creatures we do not realize we are. To them we are just a joke and they are laughing all the way to the bank.

Gone are the days of good healthy nutritious foods. Since the beginning of mass food production our lives were changed to a life of bounty and ease. For we now have more time for other things, rather then the actual preparation of our meals from scratch; from as planting the seeds, and tilling the soil to harvesting the crops, and to preparing the meal. It seems that we will never be able to sit at the table and enjoy, with our families a healthy nutritious meal from our own gardens.

This joy of a wholesome lifestyle appears to be gone forever. If only we had realized that the chemicals we placed on our crops many years ago would lead to a deficiency in the food value of our crops. We need to eat at least thirty-five or more apples today for the same value as one apple forty to fifty years ago. It is the same type of thing for all other crops grown in the fields today.

Our meats such as beef and pork are all chemically modified? Chickens and fish fare no better, grown in closed in buildings and ponds. They are not allowed to eat the natural foods they need to be a healthy source of nutrition. Chickens need to roam freely, while fish need fresh, free flowing water, but no. They too are fed chemically treated foods that end up in our bodies.

We wonder how come we are getting sickly; for most people it just doesn't click, they don't see the connection. Most people eat more then they should, at any given time and don't see the connection to the obesity problem. While many more become obese, by eating too often at fast food places and cannot fathom why they are in the state they're in.

We have gone from shopping for food at one time from the general store. To the town grocery store and now to the super huge everything you want in one place mega plaza. There you can do your shopping while waiting for a medical prescription and at the same time your car is getting new tires. With this bright new looking place we do not realize that we have lost many things. Such as the corner store meeting place where one can have a calm tranquil conversation with a friend. We are told of the great convenience to shop at the big store. Everything you want is in one place.

What we do not realize is that we are bombarded with stressful situations to our bodies. The bright lights irritate our eyes and are not healthy. Then there is the air we breathe, that was already breathed in by hundreds of other people, which help in the spreading of colds, flues and other viruses. We are bombarded with the stresses of finding a parking space.

The stress of making sure the children do not get lost and or wanting something they see but do not really need, the inability to properly budget. We see so many new and flashy widgets and gadgets that we are brainwashed into thinking we absolutely need. We walk out of there having spent more then we had intended. This proves that advertising works and works well.

Meanwhile the small ma & pa stores fade away. Jobs are lost and the economy loses. Everything is centralized for more control over the masses. We do not seem to realize that this is one very good way to lengthen the gap from the rich and poor. Think about it for a minute. The mega stores only make a few wealthy. While many little stores make many people well off.

The government loves this setup as they now get to have more control over the masses. Since now they will have to show some type of support for those that need it. That's a form of control; "big brother" is taking care of you, now you have nothing to worry about. Just sit back and vegetate while we do everything. No worries no cares. We like sheep swallow all this without realizing what is happening.

Drugs that are given to girls at twelve or thirteen years of age have a high risk of causing sterility. The excuse for these drugs is to prevent cervical cancer or some made up female problem. For some it is just another way to cause sterility. Have you ever wondered why there are so many couples incapable of having children, or of the large amount of miscarriages? Much of this is caused by foods and drugs.

Genetically modified foods, for example seedless fruits and vegetables, what are the affects to our bodies? Not to mention the loss of seeds we could use to grow more, should the need arise. We are being sterilized and so is our food source. We are being made dependent on someone in control of our food, fuel, electricity, water and our health. Personally I do not have warm fuzzy feelings of contentment knowing this.

Sure the genetically modified fruits and vegetables look and taste great, but they have had their reproductive genes removed. The seed producing gene no longer exists in them. Therefore we lose the ability to plant and grow more. There are countries where it is against the law to have more then a certain quota of original seeds (seeds prior to being genetically modified). You can not sell any produce from original seeds, this goes for any kind of seed. Ask yourself, what is wrong with this picture?

How do we really know for sure if the genetically modified foods do not serve to sterilize us or cause us to become more docile and controllable? Many will not drop the idea of sterilization until it is found to be proven one hundred percent safe.

"Holy mackerel" Martin gasped as Ronny finished. "I never knew, or even imagined all this. You sure know how to open someone's eyes". Ronny nodded knowingly, saying "I am not trying to scare anyone. I'm just trying to open your minds. To make you think, that way you will be better able to understand where, Catherine and I differ in our way of thinking and understanding of what goes on in this world. Now we can pass some of what we know on to this group, that we call our friends." Everyone clapped in appreciation, each realizing that this was the beginning of something wonderful for them.

Richie noticed several heads popping up over the fences from the neighboring yards, but said nothing. He was caught up in the spirit of the moment and realized he was learning something that most people were not aware of. Then and there he decided to learn as much as possible from Ronny; to then help as many people that he could. "Ronny" he asked, "would we be able to help others by telling them what you are teaching us?" "Of course" Ronnie replied. "Remember, though that only those that are seeking knowledge will listen to what you have to say."

"Many people are always trying to better themselves, while many more just live day to day and are content to let others tell them what to do. They do not realize the harm being done to them. Life is so simple when all you really care about are the sport scores, and who did what to who on some soap show. To Catherine and I this is about as brain dead as you can get."

Hank was visibly agitated by this remark, for he was a sports fanatic, he knew all the history of his favorite sport which was American football. Catherine nudged Ronny who quickly saw Hanks situation. "Hank you have no reason to feel uncomfortable because you are also out there playing the game. That keeps you active and your mind alive.

I am talking about all those couch potatoes who sit there for hours on end frying their brains with all the brain washing on TV. No I'm not forgetting Malcolm and Grace. They at least see their problem and try to be active, or they would not have gone swimming earlier."

Catherine announced that it was getting late, when James wanting to hear another story chimed in. "Ok James just two little one's and then we'll plan another Saturday". "Next Saturday" they all yelled in unison.

Down at the general hospital on Main St. Doctor Blair was over tired, lamenting "they just keep coming in and we can't do a thing for them."

"It must be a reaction to the drug we are using to prevent the worst from happening," replied the nurse. "It seems to be the weak and the elderly," replied Dr Blair. "The medical industry has to come up with something for these people as well or we will keep losing more every day". With a heavy heart Dr Blair sat down for a much needed rest.

He watched the tired nurses attending patients lining the hallway as all of the available rooms were overflowing. In despair he dropped his head into his hands. "How could all this get so out of control in a developed country?" As of yet, he did not know the whole truth of what or why it all happened.

"Is this related to that drug company story about George and Stan?" asked Martin. "Yes" replied Ronny and continued talking.

Ken received a phone call from his friend Kevin. He was announcing his departure from town, as he was on his way to visit his son three hundred miles away. With sadness in his voice Kevin reported the bad news to Ken. "My son Jason just called to tell me that his wife only four months pregnant lost the child." Jason's wife had been induced to deliver her stillborn infant. It was discovered during an ultra sound test that the fetus had not developed kidneys or a bladder.

The doctors advised Jason's wife that they should induce as soon as possible, for fear of placing the mother in mortal risk. The doctors also mentioned that the baby might live for two hours at most. Sadly the baby was still born, in a sense reducing the trauma to the parents.

Here is a precious life lost, but why? What caused this deformity? To many it would be called an act of God, bringing his soul back to the flock. To others it would be a punishment for the sins of the parents. Where as, in truth, it is the result of the sins of the pharmaceutical and food industries in their quest for profits. They have no conscience in regards of all the misery and death in their wake. Hell, they do not even give it a second thought.

Ronny announced, "Who here knows which industry has one of the highest salaries for its executives?" They all looked at each other, and started discussing this question among themselves. Ronny asked "any guesses?" James spoke up saying "If this is not a trick question I'll say the medical industry". "You are correct," replied Ronny.

"Wow. You're just full of these stories" remarked Jeff as Ronny finished talking.

Grace, Jen, and Alice, Richie's wife went in the house to help Catherine clean up. The boys stayed out helping Ronny clean up the deck and yard, while Malcolm's two boys put away all the pool toys. "This has been one heck of a day," Jeff said to Richie, "yep sure has, and I can't wait for next Saturday.

I wonder what else Ronny will tell us" replied Jeff. Malcolm hearing this remarked "I think it might all depend on the questions we ask." "True, true" replied Richie with a smile, "I'm already thinking of some". "So am I" Jeff said.

The following Saturday was overcast with a slight drizzle. Ronny had organized the basement games room into a make shift meeting hall so all could feel that this was actually a meeting of importance. While Catherine had organized a buffet table on the side so there would be no interruptions by having to run upstairs all the time.

Plenty of food and drinks, as well as comfortable chairs were all ready when the guests started to arrive. Ronny and Catherine were not surprised when everyone arrived at the same time, all beaming with anticipation for what they would learn.

Once all were seated Ronny sat down on a chair facing his guests. "Did you all have a good week?" All responded with varying degrees of excitement. Just then James spoke up and asked, "I have been thinking of what you said last weekend and I still don't understand what that has to do with us? Can you explain it a little more please?"

Ronny stood up saying "sure can. What do you think of a business… no an industry based on pain, discomfort, and death? It is a multi-billion if not a multi-trillion dollar a year industry that is totally dependent on illness and diseases. Let us look at this a little closer. The medical and food industries are both working together and controlled by the Food and

Drug Administration (FDA) along with a few other government endorsed administrations. Now there is a red flag!

"The food industry is, I believe, controlled by eight large corporations in all of North America who make it very difficult for smaller food manufactures to start. That way they are able to corner the market and get the larger share of the profit. This is how they reduce the competition, which is fierce, hence are able to control what goes into the processing, such as additives and preservatives, not to mention fillers.

"Now most of these additives and preservatives are very harmful to the human body. I should not forget our pets of course, for they too are a very big business and their food is just as dangerous as ours. We and our pets get sick and it all happens so slowly that most do not realize it. We do not put two and two together.

"If you have not noticed Catherine's buffet table has good quality food on it that most of you do not recognize, this is because we shop at organic and health food stores. As far as we are concerned shopping at a regular store is playing Russian Roulette". Grace leaned over to Malcolm and whispered in his ear, "so that's why the food tasted different". Malcolm nodded in agreement. She then raised her hand and asked "is that why you and Catherine look so healthy and slim?" "Yes" replied Ronny, "that plus proper exercise".

Ronny continued, "So what happens is that people get sick, or have some sort of reaction that they can't figure out why or how it happened. Things like pimples, acute gastritis now called the disease of Acid Reflux, obesity, and many other ailments and allergies. Now is the time for the medical industry to come to the rescue. We then take one form of medication or another to combat said ailments, all the while still eating and drinking what is causing it all in the first place.

"What the public is not aware of is that the medication is only to cover or sooth the illness, not to prevent or cure it. Why? If it eliminated the illness we would then stop buying that medication, pill, spray, or lotion and the pharmaceutical companies would lose money. They want a perpetual supply of patients; the last thing they want is to heal the world.

"Diseases play a large part for revenue earned by the pharmaceutical industries. That is why as long as they have it their way you will never see a cure for any type of disease, be it cancer, diabetes or any other. Sure, they will allow some news flash that something is around the corner to keep the public satisfied that they are working very hard to help us, but it always seems so very long in coming. Meanwhile, the public soon forgets the news flash and continues buying the useless and harmful drugs, suffering and dying unaware of the deception.

"Meanwhile there apparently is not enough money being generated through existing drugs and diseases. New diseases are invented practically every day in order to sell more newly invented drugs. These new drugs are hardly even properly tested, except maybe in some third world country where it is easy to hide the fatalities of test results which have gone very badly. Even then even the tests are not given enough time to prove any type of proper result whether positive or negative.

"Usually when test results show some promise of a positive nature… that apparently is good enough. Actors portraying doctors and nurses are hired to advertise these products as safe. When a profit of 200 to 300 or more percent can be made on some useless drug that more then likely will cause more harm then good can be placed on the drug store shelf, why divulge the real cure?

"I feel sick and disgusted whenever I walk in or past a grocery store or pharmacy. Since I know that a high majority of the product being sold in those places are not healthy for the human body. By that I mean the food and drink will make you ill in the long run. The drugs only mask the symptoms and do not actually heal, let alone prevent the cause. Many actually cause more medical problems so they can sell more drugs.

Just for an example, if we were to eliminate all the products containing medium to high sugar contents from the shelves. Do you know what would happen? Grace quickly picked up on this. "Half the store would be empty?" "Very close;" Ronny replied. "People often buy on impulse, pretty packaging helps stimulate sales. Also many brands do not fully list their ingredients of what is inside, often times we are misled by wording. With the example of sugar you find that there are many names for this one product alone.

"Women are treated inhumanly. A woman sees herself as truly feminine when she can proudly display full and natural breast. The medical industry has, over the years, taken that privilege away from too many women. How? With breast cancer, normal breast cancer is too slow to develop and it usually disappears naturally. So they came up with the mammogram which so obscene and medieval.

"This devise has only one true intention, and that is to squeeze the breast at about fifty pounds pressure as to actually cause damage. If you squeeze your forearm with your fingers for a few seconds you will see some sort of mark or reddish area. Think about what happens to the breast at fifty pounds pressure. Any glands that might at that time be a little inflamed will be further damaged, with a higher chance of infection leading to probable and in most instances cancer. Voila. A new cancer patient is on the books.

"Out come the knives, off come the breast. Not too far off from a butcher shop scenario. The more chopped off breast, the more money being made. Oh, and let's not forget all of the chemo that the poor woman had to go through first; lost hair, sleepless nights full of worry, then ultimately the chop off. If she survives, she is in a three percent category, which is a lie as well. The doctors, nurses, and the medical industry are praised for their glorious achievement, while they, in fact, caused it in the first place. Praise the "Pink Ribbon" and the run for finding a cure for breast cancer.

"It sickens me when for example in Canada a true hero appeared, His name was Terry Fox. After having lost a leg from cancer, he decided to raise money for a cure by running from one coast of Canada to the other. Unfortunately he died of cancer before completing this grueling endeavor. Since then millions of people have taken up the cause. There are annual Terry Fox runs all over the country, from school children to companies and banks raising funds for the cancer society.

"The sad part is Terry Fox and all the other people are just pawns used by the cancer society. Easy money for them to pocket, they do not want you to know that they have the cures, They want you to keep thinking that they are hard at work doing research, this way money keeps coming into their bank accounts. All of the people who organize and run the events such as the pink ribbon, and daffodils for cancer research are all volunteers doing the work to raise money for those greedy heartless individuals at the top.

"These volunteers and those that contribute are being used and taken advantage of. One point eight trillion dollars per year is raised just for cancer research. That does not include all other monies raised for the other diseases such as "Heart and Stroke", "Diabetes, Alzheimer's, Parkinson's Disease" and so on. Again I say too much money is being made to let the cures be made public. Many top executives have six figure salaries. This insanity must end and must end soon.

"Follow the total amount of money raised for any particular cancer fund raising event. Ask yourself this question: Where does the money end up? When you think about it, you will see that salaries must be paid to the full time staff. Note: To some of those higher up the ladder, some of these salaries are overly generous. There are advertizing costs like TV, radio, pamphlets, flyers with miscellaneous cost to these. Then there is the building maintenance along with electricity, water, phone, office supplies and such, whatever it takes to keep all this operating.

"Whatever funds that might be left would go to the research labs where the system is repeated again, salaries and funds for their operation requirements. Coming down to the actual research, what funds are left? If you don't believe then check it out for yourself.

"If the majority of the public were given the cures for most of our present diseases, then the medical industry would collapse and many people would be unemployed. In my opinion it would be better for those employed in the production of the useless and harmful junk they call medicine to lose their jobs. The prevention of further deaths and suffering of many millions would more than make up for the comparative few who would lose employment producing crap. On the other hand, they could find employment producing naturally organic healing products.

"The need for Health Insurance would be a non-issue, for treatment centers would no longer be needed. Homeopathic medicine and clinics would flourish. Prices would drop. In general people would be far healthier than today. "What about hospitals?" Shelly asked. Catherine replied, "Oh hospitals would still be needed, though they would be very different then what we see today. People still get into accidents, and little boys will still do crazy things, like breaking an arm or leg. Doctors and nurses will still be needed you see.

"As long as greedy dishonest people have the power to control medical resources, the pain, misery and needless death will never stop. They the top executives in charge of these food and drug organizations are themselves the most vicious cancers destroying humanity from the inside out. Thus they are the true cancer on society feeding on the brainwashed victims". "You are very serious about all this, hey Ronny?" Jeff asked.

"Yes I am" replied Ronny. "Ever since I found out about all this, I realized that my parents and other relatives who are now dead, as well as all of the millions who have passed away from curable diseases, were in my mind in fact murdered." "What?" James gasped.

"Yes in my mind if you hold back a cure and people die, that to me is murder. To also make a profit from it further infuriates me." Ronny slowly muttered, as he thought of his parents who would still be alive today were it not for the present medical system controlled by the FDA and the like. Catherine hugged Ronny for she knew his pain. Her eyes observed the group, she could see that what they were hearing seemed to make sense to them, "Aha" moments were occurring as faces saddened.

Just then, James asked Ronny "Hey Ronny, you keep saying that there is a cure for cancer, but you never said what it was." Ronny replied, "Yes I have haven't I? Well, in fact, from what I hear there are about three hundred of them.

If you were to get a book called "The Only Cure for Cancer" By Dr. Caldwell, you would be amazed at the amount of information that is kept hidden from the public.

"Simply go to KT Radio on the web and you will find all sorts of information for all types of problems. Mostly drug free cures, or natural drugs will be found on this site oh and you can even listen to the (Kevin Trudeau show) Ronny added.

Many in the group were busy writing this new info down for later referencing when they got home. “Finally we got some stuff to check out for ourselves” Richie whispered to Alice. Catherine overhearing this softly whispered back, “All you had to do was ask. Also don’t forget to read the book “The Only Cure for Cancer” By Dr. Caldwell. Ronny mentioned that the meeting was finished, that sometimes his emotions get the better of him. They all agreed to meet the following weekend.

Chapter Two: Governments

As everyone was seated many were wondering what the subject would be today, when Jeff stood. "Where do you get all this information from?" He asked. Well Ronny responded Catherine and I do not watch TV, like most others in fact we rarely watch it at all unless it's educational or we put in a movie for relaxation.

Most of the time we read and surf the web. Also we are members of the Global Information Network and are also members of what was once a secret society called Neo-Think@ which means a new way of thinking. Furthermore a lot is lifetime experiences and simple observation on what is going on in the world, and all that happens to others around us.

"In regards to news on TV and news papers, most of the news is one sided meaning you are told only what they want you to hear or read. Most of the real and important news is kept from the general public. Sure they "show some world events, or some sort of catastrophe, mostly stuff that does not show their true agenda.

"You are constantly force fed scenes of buildings on fire, or some bush or forest fire and people being gunned down or a police shoot out, which are constantly repeated and covered to the tiniest detail. Very rarely do you see anything of value or wonderful and these are only shown for a very short time. When did some idiot decide that the public only wants to see blood, death, and destruction?

They will also dissect the weather until you feel the heat or the raindrops. Then there are sports. More time seems to be spent on this topic than important world events. Many sports as possible seem to be mentioned, and in so much detail you almost feel that you played the game yourself. Statistics fly every which way involving players compared to other players, sometimes players who have passed away are compared in one way or another.

"Whole weekends are dedicated to watching over paid athletes play some game or other. Hockey, soccer, baseball and at the top of the list is football. Hours are spent leading up to the big game, the there's "The Game", and then hours of discussion after the game. All the while those that are watching all this are being turned into obese, alcohol saturated, brain dead minds. All to keep you away from thinking, and/or realizing what is really going on.

"This is, in my mind a devious distraction to keep you from thinking and functioning properly, to prevent you from bettering your self mentally and physically. The time wasted watching TV prevents, you from making things better for yourself and your family. We are being turned into a nation of fat bellied, beer guzzling couch potatoes with no more ambition then to reach for the chips and a cold beer. Do you think they would have a hard time taking over total control with much of the nation in the above mentioned statement? No, I don't think so!

"I am attempting to enlighten you about what the so called "authorities" are doing and planning, without going into too much detail. I am not attempting to persuade you to confront or retaliate with force. My goal is to enlighten you on how you can become aware and protect yourselves from becoming victims. So as not to be used and abused as cannon fodder, and to show others to do the same, so they can also defend themselves.

"Catherine and I are willing to explain as much as we can, but at the same time, you must be willing to read all that you can. I am not talking about comic books though they are often a source of relaxation to help with ones imagination. Many books are available to open one's mind for positive affirmations, for success in many areas of ambition that you might have. Others contain valuable information on subjects that help us through our daily lives. The internet is another source of information."

"Give us some examples", pleaded James. "Well James since you are the first to have asked for some help, and this will help the rest of you as well I suggest that you all purchase this book: ("The Natural Cures". They don't want you to know about) by Kevin Trudeau. He has also written two others that am aware of. These books will be very helpful in opening your eyes to a new world of knowledge."

Richie interrupted saying, "everything that you have mentioned so far seems to be the responsibility of the government. We need to figure out how to destroy the government and all who work there. They all seem to be against us." Ronny answered by asking if they wanted to hear another little story. All agreed.

We should not be too angry at the government as we know it. The lower level of government employee is really just doing a job. To them that is how they see it, performing a service for their country. They honestly believe their work is for the public good, for the nation to which they belong. Most do not realize much of the needless damage caused to many individuals. They do not see the wasting of valuable time and resources of the working class. Examples would be the filling out of tax forms.

Productive people find themselves standing in lines for useless permits and licenses. They have been brainwashed with the fear of breaking some little known law. Or penalties for late fees or being unlicensed for something or other, all in the name of keeping the public at bay and controlled. These government employees just blindly follow the rules set down from those above. They themselves do not realizing they are as sheep or worse, automatons.

For an example of imposed burdens on the small business, we see situations such as the following:

A small commercial sewer cleaning company has two trucks and employs his three sons. The owner of this company started off with a simple idea, to perform a service to the public while making a living. Knowing he would never become a millionaire cleaning sewers, but at least he would not be in the welfare line. Therefore he would not be a burden on society. Through his business his family would also be employed.

All was going well, money was coming in. Expenses, and taxes were being paid. Then he started receiving phone calls from different government departments. Department number one "The Ministry of the Environment" said you will now have to spend more money to have the material that you remove from the storm catch basins tested for toxins, and also the materials you remove from the ground since you use potable water while your trucks vacuum these materials into your tanks. (Now drinking water and regular dirt is now in their eyes a contaminated substance). The owner said "why don't you now sue God for contaminating the earth when it rains? Cause it's the same thing."

The same business owner then receives a second phone call, this time from W.S.I.B (a government controlled employee injury insurance agency) stating that they have now implemented a new law, that from now on all family owned business must be insured through them. The small business owner thinks about this and finds that now he must pay three times the amount for a disability insurance policy only to get a quarter of the coverage.

For the small business owner this is the straw that broke the camels back. That evening he meets with his three sons, and shortly there after his business no longer exists. Why? Because the government has stuck its nose in again to cause even more of a burden on the people whose only dream is to have some sort of an independent life. This business did not fail, or collapse through poor business practices, it was destroyed by the greed of a self serving authority, whose only ambition is to take and take from people who produce a value for society.

In short the majority of government workers are just as innocent as the rest of the population. If the majority of government workers found out the true reason for their designated responsibilities to the public, they would surly be sickened, and the whole system would probably collapse. The real guilty are those at the top. They plan privately in back room offices or golf courses the real and evil reasons for this law or that regulation. They then come up with ways to sugar coat these to fool the public as well as the pawns who work for them.

They are the power mad, the glory seekers. Their hidden agendas are not for their own constituents but for their own benefit and glory. To ensure that the general public stays at bay, obeys and pays their tithe, demanded and received by threat of force, intimidation and coercion. The government, who in turn spends it mostly without regard or responsibility for those who were robbed out of hard earned time blood sweat and tears.

Many times this money is taken off the table for food and necessities to sustain life. In reality the taxes are illegal, but of course you are not told that, and they collected through threat of force or intimidation, if you refuse to pay well its jail time. Even attempting to defend yourself is almost foolish, simply because the system will drain you financially.

Very few people have fought and won by threatening to inform the rest of the population that it is the government who is breaking the law on collecting taxes. The reason the tax collection agencies get away with it is because the public is not fully informed of their legal rights. Yet the population pays because of a longtime mindset, based on fear and intimidation. Those people who don't pay are left alone as long as they don't rock the boat.

"More companies and other small businesses disappear because of government bungling then for any other reason. What do you mean Ronny?" asked Jeff " "As I mentioned before, the governments at all levels, from the federal down to the municipal level take a piece of the action. Each level imposes its own tax and regulations, on the business. This burden restricts the movement and profit margin of a value creative enterprise. Value producers (workers) are also restricted and burdened by taxes and regulations", replied Ronny.

"This will continue until they tax the air in your lungs. There is talk that in some areas attempts are being made to charge and tax you for the water you take from your own well on your own land. They figure they can do this since they are already charging you a land tax, why not water as well.

"Government spending has gotten so out of hand, that they are constantly searching for new ways of taxing you, while at the same time preventing you from making things better for yourself, by imposing time and money wasting rules and regulations along with false taxes. Then they have the audacity to say that you are the drain on society. Why, in the hopes that you don't see that it is they who are leaching off your efforts.

"Our governments are supposed to be working for us not over taxing and coercing us through intimidation to do their bidding. We need to get back what is rightfully ours. We need to get back to 'for the people by the people'. The day is coming when a new political party that is genuinely for the people will emerge. When this day arrives, don't hold back and watch. Take action and help by voting them into office. The rewards will be well worth your votes

"Even our police departments, who we see every day, are always in patrol cars, when at one time they walked a beat and we all knew his name. Most people were not afraid or intimidated by his presence. He was there when we needed him and he was always polite and approachable. That has changed through time, now we find him more intimidating and arrogant. Now a days he/she is fixated on force and intimidation, very close in many cases to an abuse of power, by hiding behind a badge of office.

"When they have it in their minds that you are guilty, you are most often not given the chance to defend yourself and are almost immediately treated as a hardened criminal, even for the smallest of infractions. No I am not saying that every single officer is power mad, though there are a large number that are.

"Now when a patrol car stops a motorist for whatever violation, most of the time the patrol car is parked in such a way as to interrupt normal traffic flow. The officer or officers appear to see no problem with this. We are police and we can interrupt or slow the traffic as we please. This seems to be of no concern to them. Meanwhile the motorist being given a ticket for some minor traffic infraction is treated almost as a time hardened criminal.

"You are suspect to the point that you are not allowed to get out of your vehicle without their permission. This is understandable in some states where the public is allowed to carry firearms for their protection, but for many states and in Canada, it is illegal to have or carry a firearm on their person or in the vehicle without a special trip permit. Therefore, in many states and in Canada, it seems ridiculous to treat most people as criminals. But it happens.

"The logic here is that a classroom of grade four students is punished because of one student who misbehaved. You would think the officers are punishing the rest of the innocent motorist for being on the road at the same time as this criminal was. Who happened to have not come to a complete stop at a stop sign, or forgot to signal a turn, or has a burnt out light bulb.

"By this time hundreds and sometimes thousands of vehicles are affected by the slowdown, forced into a bottle neck situation because the cruiser is obstructing traffic. The busier the road, the further back and the more vehicles are affected. This is not only irritating, it is wasting fuel and telling everyone "we are the law." We do what we want, when we want so fear and be intimidated by us. So be very careful if you complain, for you too could get into trouble for interfering with the law.

"Now keep in mind, I am only talking about minor infractions here. I understand the safety issues when there is a major accident or where public safety is at stake. Yes slow the traffic down, but not for something minor.

"It would be much more considerate to the rest of the motorists, if the police somehow found a way to get the offending vehicle to the next intersection where there is less traffic, or pull as far off the road as possible. Please note: some officers actually do this, and are to be commended for their consideration to the rest of the public."

"Sounds kind of scary," replied Richie, as Ronny finished talking. "Don't worry too much Richie, one day there will be major changes to the government as we know it today. There are a lot of people in the world who are fed up with the systems that rule us, and there will be a change for the better. There is a lot of work being done under the radar. These will bring beneficial changes for the working people, those that produce values for others

"Some changes would be the reduction in taxes, allowing more money to be used for research and development for most businesses. Many useless rules and regulations, which at this time are just time and energy wasters for business, would simply vanish. These two items alone would cause a drastic reduction in costs for products and services. Start up fees would be negligible for new business ventures, allowing more new businesses to be able to grow and prosper, thereby employing more people, and therefore reducing the unemployment rates.

"Here is another example of the abuse of power, this one is municipal. Cat rescue people who love and protect cats are forced to work in an underground environment, especially when local governments are mostly dog lovers. Other wildlife rescue groups are also in the same predicament as the cat groups.

"So because of some municipal bylaws, many of the rescue groups are harassed and intimidated. This results in many animals being killed unnecessarily. This is done just to satisfy several individuals and give them the feeling of power over others, thus justifying their position on council. These people have no intention of finding a way to be helpful in a positive way. So many innocent animals are killed just to satisfy their lust for power.

"Many of the rescue groups do not give the exact count of how many animals are in their care, for fear of an invasion by the authorities, who constantly harass and intimidate the rescue groups. Here again useless laws and regulations, placed by idiotic minded people who abuse their positions to gain power over others.

"When some kind and loving people choose to dedicate themselves in the rescue and protection of wild animals, why on Earth should they be harassed and intimidated by demented power hungry idiots? These people who in and of themselves produce nothing of value to society, actually hinder any forward progress of protection and keeping the problems at a workable level.

"Let us take a break I'm starving and thirsty." No-one had to be asked a second time. Soon the food table was almost empty. Hank, wiping his mouth with a napkin, expressed his satisfaction. "This food is really good, even though it tastes a little different, I like it." "Well." replied Catherine

"I have spent a great deal of our lives investigating and learning about the healthiest foods and combinations. I look for anything healthy and nutritious for myself and to serve to those I love. You will not gain any needless weight, or suffer any ill effects from what was on this table.

When everyone was again seated, Ronny began talking again, by asking if any one had the military channel. Many responded with a yes. "How many of you look closely at what you see there?" "What are you getting at?" Jeff inquired. "Well apart from the fact that we should not totally forget the past, we should learn from it so that we do not keep making the same mistakes over and over again, expecting different results. (Einstein's interpretation of insanity by the way)

"When I observe this supposedly educational channel that shows many historical documentaries of the various wars through out history, dissecting and attempting to understand the why's and wherefores seems reasonable, to teach and explain. The commercials of course should all be thrown in the garbage bin. It is when they show programs detailing this or that top ten killing machine, be it a tank, jet, bomber, bomb or some gun, causes me to wonder.

"The military, and sections of the government, seek to perpetuate anything relating to war, or of the possibility of it. They are constantly refining weapons to keep ahead of any seen and unforeseen enemy. Inventing new weapon systems and spying equipment seems to give them a feeling of usefulness and purpose for their existence.

"All efforts, seems to be placed on how many of the enemy can be killed or maimed at one time, and from how far away. They work on weapons capable of being used by day or night, in freezing cold or other extreme weather conditions. All thought and energy is placed on how much destruction and death can be inflicted on the perceived enemy".

"Well that answered a lot of questions, I suppose you have more to say?" asked Hank "Yep I sure do," replied Ronny, who then pulled out another paper and began reading.

It has now been many years since what we have now come to know as 9/11. Prior to that 911 meant an emergency phone number. 9/11 is now synonymous with the tragic events which occurred in New York City, September 11/2001, causing the twin towers to come crashing down. How could a plane destroy a tower, when it hits near the top of that building? Did the plane fuel burn so hot as to actually melt the steel girders? Or was there something else that assisted in the destruction of these beautiful structures?

Why this particular date? These are questions that do not seem to have definite answers. Speculation abounds as to who really planned all this. Someday, the truth will be known and it will shock many of the world's citizens.

Who ever planned and implemented this event has done a masterful job of setting the blame on others to hide the true facts. Look at how the public seems to be oblivious to the destruction at the Pentagon. If you were to revue the videos of the hole in the pentagon wall minutes after the so called "plane crash", what would you see?" Hank stood and said "a fairly large round hole."

"Yes," Ronny replied, "and do you notice also that where the wings would have hit there were no signs of that let alone broken plane parts, like wheels, engines, seats or other debris? Did you also notice that the person who witnessed a military plane shoot a missile at the pentagon causing the blast site was silenced?

"People believe the fabricated story of a plane hitting the pentagon, thereby allowing the authorities telling the public "we will start a war on the terrorist for we all know who they are." Now the government has the ok to invade several countries. This in turn will cause more hatred for us and death for many innocent victims.

A great deception carefully masterminded on the world stage so as to bring about the next phase in a master plan of world dominance. The vast majority of the worlds population is easily deceived by false promises and lies through the skilful use of the media in order for the final take over. Yet many people see through these lies and deceptions and must try to let others know. They must fight diligently to spread the truth, especially when they do not have control over the media.

(Who is a terrorist?) you might ask, and "why is that person a terrorist?" What caused this person to become a terrorist? There are many reasons why. The subject is very complicated and filled with so many questions that one wonders if they will ever be answered. Poverty has often been blamed, as the main reason for this phenomenon, to keep the real truth hidden from the public mind. On the other hand, politics is actually one of the main reasons, to get another country's population stirred up enough to cause unrest then activate a change for the better.

Many people who want to change something for their own political ambitions will stir something up to cause this unrest, then go in and fix it to appear as hero's thus furthering their political goals. They will do this and then blame some other group to stir unrest somewhere else. Keep the world, fighting with one another, and there is no chance of peace.

Most terrorists, I believe are only trying to better themselves or their country and are tired of some other countries involvement into their own affairs. Other people are labeled as a terrorist simply by defending themselves from an oppressor, a group of people that see their own politicians have grown to the point of mishandling the affairs of that country and mistreating its citizens.

Then when a small group of people try to change the policy somehow and use force they are then called terrorists. This occurs in any country where the government has not treated its citizens in a proper fashion. So dissent is a factor of terrorism. Poverty plays only a minor role in causing any form of decent of a population let alone terrorism.

Meanwhile other sections of this same government is training and supplying equipment to the next set of enemy forces. This group will then eventually set in motion made up reasons for another conflict, perpetuating their war games. Why? Profits? Culling of the population?

They are sowing the seeds of misunderstanding and misinformation to the general public, thereby creating a need for their existence. There seems to be no thought or concern as to how much money is being taken away from doing good in other places, nor for how much suffering and death will be inflicted upon the innocent.

Many conflicts, of course, are really the result of power struggles of the upper elite, who use the population as pawns in their deadly chess games. In their eyes those at the bottom of the ladder or pyramid are just cannon fodder, where the one with the most expendable lives has the better chance of winning the game.

Propaganda is a very useful tool, one used to turn the citizens around to your way of thinking, turning one nation against another. The mentality set will slowly change, especially when an ideology is constantly pounded into the mind of the citizens who originally had no intention of getting involved in conflict. Lies and orchestrated events, carefully presented, can change many innocent minds into angry and vengeful automatons and will then do the bidding of the puppeteers.

"Wow" Martin said, "Is there anything else?

"Sure" answered Ronny, "here are some tidbits

"Not only are the police departments slightly power crazy, since 9/11 it has gotten very idiotic. Many Canadians, for example, wishing to go shopping at US stores are harassed at the borders, simply because they forgot the name of the shopping plaza or the address. Also even a temporary memory loss or a small slip of the tongue will get you behind bars.

"The border control officers seem to be overly zealous power mad paranoid- schitzo's. If you look at them the wrong way, you are apt to get arrested. You must cower before them, showing them, your submissive side. You are to cower in fear of their awesome powers and not to ask why, or attempt at explaining yourself or they will twist your word, to suit their suspicions of your being a highly dangerous terrorist. This is not protection. This is the utmost in harassment and embarrassment.

True terrorists have already figured out the best and safest ways across the borders. Yet the border guards are so paranoid that everyone is suspected probably even their mothers. They cajole, then, accuse, the innocent public through the threat of force and intimidation, whether they be Canadian or US citizens or visitors from another country. Now these days, if you even closely resemble a Muslim, well heaven help you.

"Let's ask ourselves, where does this paranoia that effects so many mindless people who have been given the authority to arrest, come from? Well in my opinion, and from what I have seen and heard, the real culprit here is the top level government along with its bungling departments and agencies. I will show you this list later. These departments and agencies should not even exist. They are a scar, a festering, infected, cancerous wound on society, stealing, cajoling, and then imprisoning us.

"We accused the Nazis of their cruelty and freedom stealing ways during WWII. We were led to believe that Nazism was dead, it is not. It is only wearing a different mask. It still exists along with our idea of communism, but in a way more terrible, right here in North America. Oh yes, other so called free countries are also infected.

"Do not for an instant think you are free. To the higher ups in power, you are only a mouse in a cage running nowhere on the little wheel that you think is freedom. Try taking a trip across the border, try not paying your taxes, try talking back to a paranoid officer.

"Have you ever asked yourself the question as to why so many companies have gone over-seas? Why so many manufacturing companies no longer exist in North America. Why so many people are out of work. Why so many businesses fail, and why taxes keep going up? You can thank your governments for all this plus the paranoia that is rampant throughout the country and at our borders.

This is all fueled by the media, TV, radio and the newspapers (controlled by the government and some agencies). The news you see is only what they will allow you to see. They control over 90% of the media. Fortunately there is still a small percentage of free media that we can use for as long as we can before they are gone, and if that happens we are doomed.

"The G8 Summit held in Canada in the summer of 2010 will cost the Canadian people close to a Billion dollars and three hundred and fifty Million of that is for security. $350,000,000.00 is for protection. Go figure. They are either very paranoid or are so far out in space that they think its ok and we will not even complain.

"They do not seem to realize that we are fed up with this idiotic bumbling which they have sharpened into a fine art of deception for many people who as of yet do not see. But we the enlightened, know that after spending close to a billion of our tax dollars, they will then tell us in their usual mumbo jumbo double talk language that they did not come up with any ideas on how to solve our economic problems.

"These are pretty sad results for a billion dollar two day party. The pathetic individuals which most of the population calls our leaders, cannot, will not and refuse to be of any use to the public good. Their only real reason for being where they are is to live off the fat of the land, contributing nothing to the public and smiling at us as they do nothing but take from and abuse us.

"You are urged to wake up and become aware of what is going on around you before it is too late. Look, listen, and learn, then tell your friends and families what you have found out. Spread this information to all that would listen. Our freedom is at stake here and now. The tyranny that is coming will imprison you and your country if you continue to do nothing. They will tell that all is well hoping that you never realize the truth and that they are "bleeping" you.

We are also being affected, by the release of chemicals from the high flying mostly military aircraft that are leaving behind what are known as "chemtrails". One could argue that they are getting rid of some nasty stuff by diluting it into the atmosphere. On the other hand, why do this over densely populated areas? Not to mention, this is happening on a daily basis. Don't you think then that these nasties would start accumulating after time becoming harmful to people and other living things?

The head of the snake must be cut off; then the body will die. In other words, once those at the top have fallen, or lost the grip they hold on the heads of states and other religions, the minions who serve them and have helped keep them there by doing their bidding will no longer have leadership. Only then will this corrupt system fall, freeing the planet after 2300 years of imposed lies and deceit. Some of the followers will probably perish, but many others will themselves discover new found freedoms.

"What are examples of the rest of the body?" Hank inquired. Ronny reached into a large briefcase and removed a sheet of paper and showed it to the group.

USA AGENCIES		CANADIAN AGENCIES	
IRS	Internal Revenue Service	CRA	Canada Revenue Agency
FTC	Federal Trade Commission	CTCS	Canada Trade & Commissioner Service
FDA	Food & Drug Administration	HC, HPFB, CFIA	Health Canada, includes: HPFB Health Products Food Branch & CFIA; Canadian Food Inspection Agency
EPA	Environmental Protection Agency	EC	Environment Canada
SEC	Securities & Exchange Commission USA	SEC	Securities & Exchange Commission Canada
DEA	Drug Enforcement Administration	DEA, RCMP	Drug Enforcement Administration Royal Canadian Mounted Police
FBI	Federal Bureau of Investigation	CSIS	Canadian Security Intelligence Service
INS	Immigration & Naturalization Services	IRBC	Immigration & Refugee Board of Canada

ATF	Alcohol Tobacco Firearms	PSC	Public Safety Canada
CIA	Central Intelligence Agency	CSIS, CISC, & SIRC	Canadian Security Intelligence Service, Criminal Intelligence Service Canada & Security Intelligence Review Committee
NSA	National Security Agency	CSE	Communications Security Establishment

"These are some of the agencies that have caused many innocent people to suffer needless pain and sorrow. They are the cause of what we see as restrictions to many of our so called freedoms which we think we have but in reality do not. Any one who thinks otherwise is seriously mistaken. These systems were originally set to protect us.

"Over the years they veered away from protection to self preservation, causing more harm then good by setting their own agendas, and coming up with reasons to stay in power. They have the backing of the government, and are part of the government, yet most often act with their own policies and agendas. Also remember the "World Health Organization" (WHO) is not the kind friend that you are led to believe. They also have an agenda on culling of the world's population.

"Why is it right and ok for politicians to get severance pay when leaving office, while there is so much unemployment? Also, why don't all regular people get a severance when they get laid off except for some chosen few? What on God's green Earth make politicians so special? This type of thing just flaunts stupidity and greed right into the face of the general public.

"We can only hope that if and when the existing government system changes to a more people-friendly and protection only system, these agencies will no longer exist, freeing us of many ills and tribulations, not to mention allowing us to keep more of our hard earned money in our pockets. Now keep in mind, what I am saying here is that we, the people, do not control them. They, attempt to control us.

"Were these agencies set as businesses, where we had the choice to choose their services or not, then that would be a different story. But we have no choice in what policies they come up with and employ to cause us grief. A true and honest business will work to satisfy our needs, so as to be successful, and prosper. A business that does not satisfy us will soon perish. So it would be in the best interest of any business to satisfy its customers in order to flourish.

"Most governments are under the impression that the money in your pocket does not actually belong to you. They are just allowing you the privilege to use it. We all believe that, as we are paying the mortgage on our dream home, that it will be ours when we are finished. Try this out sometimes, don't pay your property taxes for a year or so and see what happens. Do not be surprised if you find yourself homeless in a very short while, thrown out of the home you thought was yours.

"By rights since the house is paid for, you would think you could just pass it onto whomsoever you wished to upon your death. In many areas this is not allowed, either your estate is sold off, or the inheritor must pay a portion plus the appropriate taxes on something that has been taxed to death for years. Government has made our lives so complicated, through money grabbing and time wasting, we are wrapped in red tape all our lives

"When the government decides that it wants what you think belongs to you, then you're in for a major headache. Court cases, lawyer's fees, not to mention uncalled for time off of work just to defend and try to protect what is yours. You bought it, worked hard to pay for it. They, did what? To, make it easy for you get and pay for it? And they think they have the right to take it if you encounter financial difficulties. Which they, more then likely had a hand in causing.

"Let us change the subject and talk about something else." Catherine said as she stood up to go grab a drink from the table.

Some web sites to check for more detailed information

http://inflation.us/videos.html

http://www.brasschecktv.com/page/847.html

http://www.youtube.com/watch?v=nKsgOyO5Ntw&NR=1

http://www.stockpilefood.com/

http://www.davidickebooks.co.uk/index.php

http://media.ktradionetwork.com/media/images/coldwell/coldwell.html

http://www.ktradionetwork.com/

http://www.youtube.com/watch?v=c6SqHXrNE-0

http://www.globalhealthfreedom.org/

http://www.youtube.com/watch?v=_gWmVtn5JsA

Chapter Three: Religions

"Ronny, what is your view on religions?" inquired Shelly.

"Well, religions have been more destructive then constructive throughout history. Meaning they have caused more death, pain, and misery then actual good. By that I mean if you do not believe in God the way I do, you are wrong and most often will be punished through death and destruction.

"If all religions had since their conception, implemented this simple philosophy 'We Are All One', or even better 'Ours is not a better way, ours is merely another way', then there possibly would not have been so much ignorance based on superiority of one's own religion. All would have been allowed to believe in their own way, and therefore there would have been less death and destruction through- out history." Ronny pulled out another sheet of paper and began telling another little story.

Religions, in their own right, are not the total evil that we understand many of them to be. The problem arises from a few individuals. Those with the power of persuasion, the golden tongue, the sharp minds, the evil hearts who want nothing more than power and glory for themselves. These people misuse and misinterpret the religious words for their own benefit.

They have the uncanny ability to persuade and brainwash many individuals who would have otherwise been good and productive persons in society and the world. These people have now been turned into brainless, unthinking, no conscience automatons, doing the bidding of the evil minded leader.

Throughout the ages, with the beginning of Christianity and Islam to name two of the curses on humanity, millions upon millions of people have been murdered, mutilated or sent into lives of misery all in the name of a man-made idea of what God wants. If these religions tell to us not to kill, to treat others as we would like to be treated, then why, oh why do so many millions die in the name of God?

The lives of these many productive people, who could have made this world a better place to be, are snuffed out. The mindless automatons, led by an evil, demented power and glory seeking sub-humans simply wish to destroy all that is good. It seems to appear to us that they cause all this death, pain and misery just for the hell of it.

Such a waste of the mind and precious productive lives lost to us. These atrocities continue up to this day and age, for evil dislikes good. The ultimate goal for these governments and religious leaders is to have total control over masses of slave like automatons whose only purpose in life would be to serve with unquestioning loyalty, to glorify the chosen few.

The chosen few would then rule with total and undisputed power forever. Imposing misery and suffering on us for it makes them feel all powerful. Their only goal is to take our rights to travel freely, our ability to think for ourselves, and be happy and productive. Productive only for them, for it will make them happy, not us.

"Religions have caused much suffering and confusion while trying to benefit humanity, with the right ideas but the wrong process, causing some type of guilt or other. The attitude of 'it's our way or the highway'. Your way is wrong. Our way is right." Martin stepped in at this point asking. "Where do you get these ideas from?"

Ronny answered, "well a lot had to do with my own personal upbringing and also what I have read throughout my life that has caused me to think the way I do today. It is all a learning process, to grow spiritually and mentally. I do not mean spiritually as in a religious sense but in knowing myself at a higher level.

"Of the many books that I have read on the subject of religions, there is one such author that I would introduce at this time, for he is one that is easily understood by most people with an opened mind. He has written six books that I am aware of, and they are the trilogy of 'A Conversation with God' and two additional books titled, 'The New Revelations' and 'Friendship with God' By Neale Donald Walsch.

"These books give people a new and fresh way of looking at the concept of religion and how we view our relationship with God. Many who are locked into one religious reality will have a hard time reading this material. In my opinion, they are at a loss in the freedoms that are and will be enjoyed by those who see and understand what Neale Donald Walsch is trying to say. Those that believe only the prophets of old are the ones to be listened to have placed themselves in a box that is very difficult to get out of. They have closed their eyes to any other possibility.

"In truth there have been many prophets through the ages, just as important to us as the old ones, Yet, we believe that the prophets of long ago are the only ones who were able to communicate with God. In reality we all have that gift, but are afraid to use it, or even believe it for fear of some sort of blasphemy. We believe we are not worthy to talk directly to God. These ideas are rooted deep within us, placed there by religious dictates from ancient times.

"I am not biased to any particular religion. You have the right to your own beliefs. My argument here is that we are prisoners while being stuck in one. In other words, all those with differing beliefs should be allowed to practice what and how they choose. To have free choice, rather then forcing anyone to believe what you believe.

"If you are not of the Christian faith, you will not go to Heaven, only to Hell or purgatory. If you are not Catholic yet still of a Christian faith, such as Baptist, Lutheran, Mormon, etc, you still will not go to Heaven. Each branch of the Christian faith believes that only they will go to heaven.

Talk about narrow minded thinking, the root of segregation leading to animosity of others.

"Also, each of the other non-Christian religions believes that they are the only true faith, each with their own definition of a Heaven or final resting place for the soul or spirit, Valhalla comes to mind as an example. In a nut shell, as I have stated before and will again, is that all religions and yes governments, work hard at keeping us separate and apart from our fellow man.

"This causes much animosity and prejudice, which leads to hatred and resentment, then anger. Then it is just a small step to conflict, resulting in many deaths through wars. If they do not conform, you feel they must be punished or they must die for not believing the same as you. We are not mass produced from the same mold like robots, cars, or coffee cups. We are all individuals with different tastes, ideas and beliefs.

"Here is where the beneficial opportunities would arise. Men with differing backgrounds and ideas could brainstorm together to make something better. Be it a better way to build something, or a brand new idea. Ultimately man would be working together on a massive project to trade goods and ideas between countries without any restrictions.

"I have talked to many people who have stopped practicing the religions they were born into, and have just decided to believe in a God that is just and demands nothing from us. This God has everything there is to have, for He/She created all there is in all the universe, including us, has given us the gift of free choice to decide what we will or will not do for him.

Yet we are all a part of God and will return there at the ending of our physical bodies. God is neither male nor female, we could say the yin and yang of all that there is. We are all part of God while at the same time we are God, all linked to each other, yet separate from each other.

"We are all one family, from the first human to the last human, and every one in between. We are all linked through time and space." "Wait a minute here," interjected Martin, "You are speaking heresy, and this is blasphemy." Ronny retorted by saying, "there-in lays the major problem of man and religions. You Martin and the rest of the religious people are quick to judge when someone speaks their own minds on ideas that do not agree with yours. This leads to misunderstands and is the cause of wars.

"I was asked, where do I get these ideas from and I was explaining my own thoughts, yet you retaliated, assuming I was putting yours down. Do you understand now why, in my opinion, that religions have caused much of the pain and death through out our history?" Martin shyly apologized and sat back down.

"It is my understanding that God neither wants, nor needs, anything from us. According to most religions, He has given us free choice. Why then should we be punished when we did not do something His way? The idea of God punishing us for something or other is a man made idea.

"The leaders of most religions use that ploy to get us to tow the line and do as they say. In order for us to obey, these lies were added to the bible and other religious books so that the masses would obey the will of the few leaders. This is where the major misuse of religion comes from.

"Most religions have many powerful truths that, when listen to and acted upon, would bear great things for the people. It is when these are twisted around and mangled do they cause great harm. Unfortunately this has been our history. The works and words of Jesus, Buddha, Muhammad and others have been twisted to suit some very evil men, and we, the innocent have paid the price.

"Every so often we see or hear reports of scrolls being discovered in caves. Then there is a large and intensive investigation as to what is written on the scrolls. Has anyone ever heard of any result from these investigations?" Silence, since no one could actually answer yes. Ronny went on "does it not strike you as odd or weird that there is no other mention afterwards?" Hank stood up saying, "Cause, they are hiding some truths that would disrupt the status quo." "Well said," remarked Ronny.

Martin raised his hand, as he stood up saying, "this is all beginning to make sense now." At that moment, Catherine stepped forward saying, "can I say a few words of my own?" Martin sat down and Ronny stepped back to allow Catherine center stage.

Catherine began telling her story.

Religions in their earliest beginnings were pure and honest, bestowing goodness to all people. The words of wisdom from Jesus, Buddha, and others were then in their purest forms and intent to enlighten the people. But, unfortunately, these precious jewels of wisdom were twisted and bent out of shape by fanatical self-serving men whose sole purpose was to gain control over the masses.

Much of the truth was, and is still, kept hidden to keep us in line. Such lies and deceit have become imbedded in our psyche after almost two thousand years, and has become known as the twenty three hundred year old deception, used by a few to rule the many. Turning the masses into followers, told not to think for themselves, and made to feel guilty if they thought of other ideas on their own, kept in ignorance. Bringing about what we now call the (Dark Ages).

Martin's wife Shelly interrupted at this point asking, "Catherine, first you mentioned two thousand years, then you say twenty three hundred years, that's a difference of three hundred years from the time of Jesus. What gives here?" Catherine did not waver in her answer. My apologies Shelly, I have forgotten that you and Martin do not know the many details that Ronny and I have discovered throughout our lives. So Ronny or I will explain the twenty three hundred years deception later. Let me continue for now though, okay Shelly?" Shelly agreed and sat down.

Religion per say is beneficial for most people. It is in the way that it is used by those in power that becomes detrimental. When religion is used the wrong way, which is for ones own corrupted benefit, causing the suffering or lost freedoms by others are the main problems we have. Spreading lies and distorted truths as facts that must be believed and adhered to at all cost, or the vilest of punishments will befall you. If you do not believe or obey our teachings you will be severely punished or killed.

Varying religions have bilked the people of wealth and happiness throughout the ages. Not only that, they have stunted the genuine spiritual growth of the majority of people. The masses are kept in a virtual prison of guilt and fear, by being brainwashed into believing that they must follow a higher authority that knows what is best for them.

You are told that you are not capable in making your own judgments. You must obey, follow, and conform to our way like in the Catholic religion, or you will be excommunicated. Meaning you're no longer in the herd (of sheep), sent out to deal with the wolves on your own.

This idea of being sent out on your own scared many innocent people so much that they've conformed out of fear. If they had been on their own they would have found the truth. Some people did indeed discover these truths and were never seen again when they tried to spread the word.

Guilt is a man-made word originally used to control the ignorant and uneducated. The peasants were taught guilt as evil, a feeling of not obeying some imposed law or edict, and that a terrible punishment would follow. Fearing to be treated as a criminal kept many in line, therefore committing as few sins as possible.

Fear was instilled into them, so that they would realize they would loose their place in Heaven and would go straight to Hell (another made up word to control the masses) You are nothing, a speck, sinfull, not good, you must pray and seek mercy, and must do everything a certain way or you will not gain entry into Heaven. God will punish you forever, if should you stray.

Apart from the guilt and fear imposed on the masses, they had to give to the churches a tithe, mostly in the form of money or services. Thus great churches and cathedrals were built, and the priests, and bishops, and such became very wealthy, as they lived at the expense of the productive individuals. Who promised everything, but gave nothing. Who took and took and gave little if anything back.

"My God," Martin and Shelly pronounced in unison. "We never really heard it said that way." "Ronny and I have only just scratched the surface."

replied Catherine. "There are many horror stories that can be told from throughout the ages of atrocities caused by religions.

"For an example, when Christopher Columbus discovered the Americas while searching for a sea route to China. As Columbus landed on the first island in the Caribbean, it was the beginning of the end for many civilizations that existed beyond this island at the time. For Columbus brought with him what was to be a curse causing much death and misery.

"That thing was missionaries, monks of Christianity whose goal was to christen as many people as possible, to show them the one and only God. Those that refused were brutally killed, and the rest fell into place out of fear for their own lives. These missionaries obviously forgot, or were not told about freedom of choice. They would not allow paganism to continue.

"Untold numbers of natives would die either by refusing to be baptized or of disease spread by the Spaniards. Oh, and many more were killed by the Spanish in their search for gold and silver. I can mention many other instances of such atrocities throughout history," Catherine concluded.

"Surely you must have some positive opinions on organized religion?" pleaded Shelly. "Yes we do replied," Ronny, "would you like us to quote some?" "Yes," answered Martin.

"First you must understand that God will not punish you for doing something that you feel is wrong. Why? It is because He gave you free will, and therefore punishing you for something goes against everything. If one is punished for using what was given, then where is the logic in that? It makes no sense, yet that is what religions teach. Backwards logic.

"Here I would like to quote from the book 'The New Revelations' By Neale Donald Walsch where Mr. Walsch explains how we could better relate our religious beliefs to others.

> AS WE SEEK TO CREATE HARMONY IN OUR WORLD,
> WE THE UNDERSIGNED, HEREBY COMMIT TO
> TAKING THE FIVE STEPS TO PEACE

1. We acknowledge that certain old beliefs about Life and about God are no longer working.
2. We acknowledge that there is something we do not understand about God and about Life, the understanding of which could change everything.
3. We are willing for new understandings of God and Life to now be brought forth, understandings that could produce a new way of life on this planet.
4. We are willing to explore and examine these new understandings, and if they align with our inner truth and knowing, to enlarge our belief system to include them.
5. We are willing to live our lives as a demonstration of our beliefs.

State for example that you were to say, God is the beginning and the end, all that there is has been and ever will be. Also that we are part of God and God is part of us, we are one yet individual. Now let us compare this to the concept of the universe. God is the Universe; the Universe is God, one and the same. The ultimate power called Love which is God.

God created the universe and all that exists within it. We then are creators of our own reality. We have the power to express and create by following the laws that regulate the process of personal creation. We then express our lives through:

1. The energy of attraction, which gives you power.
2. The law of opposites, which gives you opportunity.
3. The gift of wisdom, which gives you discernment.
4. The joy of wonder, which gives you imagination.
5. The presence of cycles, which gives you eternity.

You could call this process God or the universal power. To me they are differing words for the same concept. This is a very complex system it is God being the universe being God. This is the process that produces the expression called life.

Think of this as a circle. The circle of life producing life's expressions and experiences, causing one thing to lead to another then another and so on. It is a never ending cycle of expression and experiences. Life as it is created is the process, while life as it appears is the expression, and life as it affects us is the experience.

"We determine how it affects us, either knowingly or most often unknowingly, and it is not understood by most people. All things are in the cycle, everything is here and not here at the same time. This is the law of the universe or if you want God, these two words represent one and the same idea or concept.

Ronny continued by adding, "I have read the eight books that I am aware of written by Neale Donald Walsch. These books were introduced to me by my sister. They have clarified many doubts, mysteries and questions I had pertaining to there ever being a God or higher power. So much has been explained in an easy to understand manner, easily grasped by anyone searching for some answers to questions of faith.

"Mr. Walsh is a master in his own right. Therefore, I strongly urge everyone to read his books with an opened mind. There is much wisdom within the pages of his books."

Ronny concluded by saying, "when you read these books by Neale Donald Walsch you will gain so much more understanding of God and of religions."

Richie noticed that every time they meet in Ronnie's back yard, there are more and more people quietly listening to Ronny and Catherine speak. Eventually many invited themselves, bringing their deck chairs and food, just to listen and observe. These self-invited guests were careful not to disturb the original group. Ronny and Catherine would acknowledge them as they arrived. They would smile back in return, and seemed to be grateful for being allowed to stay and listen.

As Richie sees this, he thinks to himself. (This group is growing bigger all the time, maybe Ronny is right that the world can and will change for the better. It has to start somewhere, why not this backyard, then to many more backyards?)

Richie then asked Ronny this question. "Ronny are there others who are trying to explain these things to other people like you and Catherine are doing?" "Yes. Many are talking about this like we are here. Some are writing books to spread the word and others are, on, what you could say underground radio, while still more use the internet. The more famous ones give live seminars and talks.

"Here are some more quotes from Neale Donald Walsch

"Religion is our conscious or unconscious response to the beckoning Light. Religion is our firm belief in the lofty experiences of our predecessors. Religion is our great satisfaction in our glorious past.

Spirituality is in the aspiring heart. Spirituality is of the liberating soul. Spirituality is for the fulfilling and immortalizing God."

Tire not of seeking the truth, nor of finding it"

Reference Materials:
"Conversation with God" Book One
"Conversation with God" Book Two
"Conversation with God" Book Three
"The New Revelations"
"Friendship with God" an uncommon dialogue
"Happier then God
"When Everything Changes" change everything
By Neale Donald Walsh;
www.nealedonaldwalsch.com

Chapter Four: Women's Rights Throughout History

BEING A LITTLE SHY JEN asked a question in a very low voice that was barely audible to any one else except Catherine. Catherine quickly asked Jen to repeat her question. Nervously Jen stood up and began speaking. "Jeff here says that men are and have always been better then women. That all men are far superior over all women and women are servants to men". Aghast at hearing this Catherine marched right up to Jeff and looked him in the eye, saying "I hope you don't really believe that."

Jeff was visibly nervous as he mumbled for words that would not come. The rest of the group was also visibly shaken at what they had heard. Feeling so many eyes on him, Jeff announced that this was how his father had trained him. "Well your father was very wrong," was the next thing Catherine said, but remained calm, realizing how young Jeff was and that how easily influenced he seemed to be.

To break the impending tension Ronny quickly interrupted by announcing:

Think about it men, we have had the run of the planet from the beginning. Males ruled from the times of living in the bush to roaming the plains of Africa. Onwards, we ruled while painting murals in the caves of Europe, and eventually settling down and forming communities around the world. There we built great monuments to our masculinity and egos, as well as great tombs so that we would be remembered after our deaths.

Our societies grew and flourished right up to the present day. You might say that this is all nice and dandy, but upon reflection, what do we see? We caused nothing but pain misery, death, and destruction. Our forward progress was slowed due to wars and male testosterone. It has, so far, been a rollercoaster ride of ups and downs of build and destroy, birth and death through battle. Million, upon millions of lives wasted, along with all the accumulated knowledge that is possibly forever lost.

Now if the universal mind is indeed real then there is a possibility that this lost knowledge has been retrieved, although at some later date. The fact still remains of the many delays in forward movement.

Many would argue that because of the need for wars humanity has made many great strides in technology. Better metals for swords and spears, eventually cannons and many other fine machines of war. Each side bent on creating and building, better and more efficient ways to kill and destroy. The warlords argue, we would not be where we are today, if it were not for the many fine advancements in the technologies of war.

Let us use our imagination at this point and say that there had never been any wars. Where would we be today? Now keeping in mind, all of the people that have died because of war had survived. All the accumulated knowledge would have been used and built upon. Since man, by nature, is a creator and is basically honest and good. Where would the level of technology have taken us?

We would very possibly be exploring distant galaxies, controlling the elements of nature, perhaps living thousand year life spans or more. We would have been able to use the Earth's resources in a much more positive manner. Possibly better yielding crops without the need of genetic engineering (the jury is still out on that one). The air would be much less polluted; many wonderful machines would have been invented.

The planet would not be as messed up as it is now, lands destroyed by bombs. Whole sections of this world would be safer, if it were not for all the land mines, still buried and forgotten. Think also of the ships that have been sunk. Their cargo gone to waste, and the lives lost, and lastly lands still uninhabitable due to nuclear and hydrogen bomb testing.

So the idea here is if women were to run the governments, or at least given an equal say in policy making, there would definitely be less strife and wars. Why? Women, by their nature, are the caretaker of life. Women give us life by giving birth, feeding, and loving us.

They have less reason to kill and destroy, for that, defeats the purpose of their being. I am not saying for women only in government, the responsibility should be shared equally. The voices and opinions of women should have the equivalent value. We share this world together.

Contrary to the belief of many men out there, the brain and mind of women is equal to that of men. Despite the very unique qualities for both sexes brain functions are virtually the same therefore not only do they deserve, but demand the right to be of equal partners, standing side by side, not the man in front of the woman. By doing so, the rewards of happiness and achievements are multiplied.

We, the males of our societies, must strip away the prejudice that we have long carried in our minds about women. We must shed our ego, being on top of the ladder, having dominance over woman, as only a servant in our lives. We are partners and should act as such, to consider and recognize our strengths, weaknesses, our diversity with this positive attitude the rewards are greatly enhanced for all.

Catherine interjected by saying.

Both sexes are by, nature, opposites. The Yin and Yang, complimenting each other as nature intended. We need to recognize each other's strengths and weaknesses. If man had allowed women more education and more say in public events, there would have definitely been less bloodshed and destruction.

The idea that women are to be dominated and subservient to man stems from, and this is only my opinion, from the idea of man. By and large men have more body weight and muscle. He was the hunter, provider, and protection of the smaller, weaker females, and to a degree, he still is today. The women would perform the menial tasks of skinning animals, cooking and raising the young. When a male wanted a female he would simply grab her, and have his way with her.

Male dominance continued from there, and eventually the mindset was established, that males were smarter. For thousands of years, and only through ignorance and the need for control man had degraded women to the level of slave, servant, and property. Many women were cruelly punished for simple misdeeds often caused by another male.

Religious idealism also played a major rule in the cruelty to women. Religious leaders simply brainwashed the men into believing that women had no soul and deserved no better treatment then a dog, the men obeyed for fear of going to Hell. Fortunately through time the abuse of women began to lessen, though there are some cultures that continue to this day treating women as lower than low.

Ronny then said.

The last one hundred years have seen major turning points in women's rights and freedoms. I am sure we will be grateful for this in the near future. Many great and wonderful things have been brought to us from the minds of women. Our world is, by far, a better place for us because of their fortitude, perseverance and stamina.

Still, there is much work to be done before the world can say males and females are truly equal, on the same level playing field. But let us not forget our differences, our Yin and Yang, for it is necessary for our survival, happiness, health, and prosperity. Together, hand in hand, we can accomplish many great and wonderful things.

There have been many wonderful inventions thought of by women in the earlier part of the twentieth century. These still, benefit us to this day unfortunately many of these inventions required a man's name on the patent in order for it to be accepted by society at that time.

"Some examples," Ronny continued, "Of ideas turned into inventions are the hairpin, the very first labor saving device called the washing machine, the sticky note, the paper clip, the cloth pin for hanging laundry outside on the line, the safety pin originally for babies diapers, to name a few. Did you notice that most of the above ideas were because women were on the front lines requiring these labor saving devices?" "Necessity is the mother of invention," Richie injected. "Precisely," Ronny replied.

"There have been many great women throughout history who have achieved greatness. What we fail to realize is that they had to work twice as hard as a man to receive the same respect. Especially within the last two hundred years they had to endure much hardship to reach the top of whatever field they embarked on. Today there are many more women than before who are in positions of power. This is proof positive that they are not brain-dead sex objects, truly on the same level as men intellectually.

Walking over to Ronny and grabbing his hand Catherine continued, saying

Prior to the Dark Ages, women enjoyed many freedoms that they are just now getting back. It is very sad that much was lost through religious persecutions. Distorted views of a supposedly loving God, demanding absolute obedience from women, as a slave, or property, having no rights whatsoever, even considered a mindless creature having no soul. A dog had more respect.

The fear and ignorance of man living in those early years of the dark ages caused much pain suffering and death for many innocent women. If a woman had the apparent ability to heal and help others (simply because she had love in her heart) she was considered as a witch or possessed by the devil.

Men, in their fear and ignorance, would torture and/or kill her as a witch or blasphemer, simply because she showed some semblance of intelligence, and therefore was a servant of the devil. The concept of superstition had evolved to more complex levels during this period.

Due to the ignorance of the Dark Ages, ethics, and dogma, man has been cheated out of the ecstasy derived from female companionship and compassion. For whatever pathetic reasons, men in power long ago decreed women to be of lower stature then men. They turned off the tap of happiness and joy, and most of all, the giving back of truly honest love to her man.

In those dark days, man did not realize why he was so sad, angry, and miserable. Still he obeyed his authorities, not realizing that those who governed were the root cause of his woes, unhappiness and unfulfilled life. Religious ignorance caused over a thousand years of misery and useless wars.

The love, the true, honest, love of a woman is one of the greatest gifts a man can receive. The love of children, family and friends are all also important, but the love of a woman is on a level of its own. It is the one love that unifies two halves to form a single unit. This single unit of two halves therefore has the ability to achieve more, since it is more powerful by having four arms, two minds, and one commitment.

Man's failure in keeping the love is when he feels it will always be there. This is a grave mistake for many men, and he should/must work to keep her love alive.

So many men fail here in many ways. Some examples would be:

1. Lying too often.
2. Not being open in communication.
3. Having affairs.
4. Physical and mental abuses
5. Mind games.
6. Alcoholism and/or drugs
7. Forgetfulness of important details and events.
8. Thinking only of himself (self centered)
9. Not being aware or caring for her needs. It takes two to have a loving relationship.

Catherine continued saying, "the list that Ronny just quoted goes for women as well. Since women can be guilty of the same things, often out of frustration or revenge."

Jeff, who was still standing through all this, looked as if he had been branded as something evil. Every one felt sorry to see him standing there looking the way he did, till finally Catherine announced that Jeff was not guilty of any crime, and that he had only been mislead by ignorance.

Jeff had grown up observing his father's treatment of his mother. He constantly heard the insults and humiliations, hearing him saying she was good only for making babies, cooking supper, and nothing else. Unfortunately, she through time, had accepted and believed it.

"It stops here," Jeff announced and turned to Jen and apologized for all he had said and done. Jen wrapped her arms around him then kissed him passionately. Then the room erupted with every one clapping then hugging. They were all greatly aware of having received very valuable insights this day.

Destroying something that is old and unsafe is totally different to destroying something of value for the sheer thrill of it, or an act of violence or of war. So much good has been destroyed by man, mostly based on ignorance, greed or hatred, often stirred up by misinformation or fear. Destroying old, worn out useless laws and ideas and replacing them with love and understanding for each other is necessary for our growth and happiness.

Here are some examples of women throughout history. This list was taken off the web. You can check this out for yourselves, and read some of their biographies.

The following material was taken off the web from the site listed here.

www.biographyonline.net/.../women-who-changed-world.html

50 Women who changed the World

1. Sappho -570BC

One of the first published female writers. Much of her poetry has been lost but her immense reputation has remained. Plato referred to Sappho as one of the great 10 poets.

2. Cleopatra 69 -30 BC

The last Ptolemic ruler of Egypt. Cleopatra sought to defend Egypt from the expanding Roman Empire. In doing so she formed relationships with 2 of Rome's most powerful leaders Marc Anthony and Julius Caeser. These relationships have been depicted in Romantic terms, although in reality they may have been political alliances.

3. Mary Magdalene 4 BC - 40AD

The historical facts surrounding Mary Magdalene are shrouded in speculation. However accounts from the Gospels and other sources suggest Mary Magdalene was one of Jesus' most devoted followers. It is said she was a women of "ill repute" but according to the Gospel of Mark and Luke her pure devotion to Christ earned her complete forgiveness. Mary Magdalene stood near Jesus at his crucifixion and was the first to see his resurrection.

4. Boudicca 1st Century AD

Boudicca was an inspirational leader of the Britons. She led several tribes in revolt against the Roman occupation. Initially successful her army of 100,000 sacked Colchester and then London. Her army was eventually completely destroyed in battle by the Romans.

5. Hildegard of Bingen 1098-1179AD

Mystic, author, and composer, Hildegard of Bingen lived a withdrawn life, spending most of her time behind convent walls. However, her writings, poetry, and music were revelatory for the time period. She was consulted by Popes, Kings, and influential people the time. Her writings and music have influenced people to this day.

6. Eleanor of Aquitaine 1122-1204

The first Queen of France. Two of her sons, Richard and John went on to become Kings of England. Educated, beautiful and highly articulate, Eleanor influenced the politics of western Europe through her alliances and influence over her sons.

7. Joan of Arc 1412-1431

The patron saint of France, Joan of Arc received "heavenly visions" giving her the inspiration to lead the French in revolt against the occupation of the English. An unlikely heroine; at the age of just 17 the diminutive Joan successfully led the French to victory at Orleans.

Her later trial and martyrdom on false premises only heightened her mystique.

8. Mirabai 1498-1565

Born to a privileged Hindu family Mirabai broke with the conventions of society to live the life of a mystic and devotee of Krishna. For her unconventional lifestyle her family tried to kill her, but on each occasion were unsuccessful. Her bhajans (poetry) and songs helped revitalise Devotional Hinduism in India.

9. St Teresa of Avila 1515-1582

Mystic and poet. St Teresa of Avila lived through the Spanish inquisition but avoided been placed on trial despite her mystical revelations. She helped to reform the tradition of Catholicism and steer the religion away from fanaticism.

10. Catherine de Medici 1519-1589

Born in Florence, Italy Catherine was married to the King of France at the age of 14. On the death of her husband she became Queen mother to her 3 sons. She was involved in interminable political machinations seeking always to increase the power of her favoured sons. This led to the disastrous St Bartholomew's Day Massacre in which up to 50,000 Huguenot's were killed.

11. Elizabeth I 1533-1603

Queen of England during a time of great economic and social change, she saw England cemented as a Protestant country. During her reign she witnessed the defeat of the Spanish Armada leaving Britain to later become one of the world's dominant superpowers.

12. Catherine the Great 1729-1796

One of the greatest political leaders of the eighteenth century. Catherine the Great was said to have played an important role in improving the lot of the Russian serfs. She placed great emphasis on the arts and helped to cement Russia as one of the dominant countries in Europe.

13. Mary Wollstonecraft 1759-1797

Mary Wollstonecraft wrote the most significant book in the early feminist movement. Her tract "A Vindication of the Rights of Women" laid down a clear moral and practical basis for extending human and political rights to women. A true pioneer in the struggle for female suffrage.

14. Jane Austen 1775-1817
One of the most popular female authors, Jane Austen wrote several novels, which remain highly popular today. These include "Pride and Prejudice", "Emma", and "Northanger Abbey". Jane Austen wrote at a time when female writers were very rare. Most of her early books were written under a pseudonym. She paved the way for the next generation of female writers.

15. Harriet Beecher Stowe 1811-1896
Harriet Beecher Stowe was a life long anti slavery campaigner. Her novel "Uncle Tom's Cabin" was a best seller and helped to popularise the anti slavery campaign. Abraham Lincoln would later remark her books were a major factor behind the American civil war.

16. Queen Victoria 1819-1901
Presiding over one of the largest empires ever seen Queen Victoria was the head of state for most of the nineteenth century. Queen Victoria became synonymous with the period symbolising propriety and middle class values. Queen Victoria sought to gain an influence in British politics whilst remaining aloof from party politics.

17. Florence Nightingale 1820-1910
By serving in the Crimean war Florence Nightingale was instrumental in changing the role and perception of the nursing profession. Her dedicated service won widespread admiration and led to a significant improvement in the treatment of wounded soldiers.

18. Susan B. Anthony 1820-1906
Susan Anthony campaigned against slavery and for the promotion of women's and workers rights. She began campaigning within the temperance movement and this convinced her of the necessity for women to have the vote. She toured the US giving countless speeches on the subjects of human rights.

19. Emily Dickinson 1830 – 1886

One of America's greatest poets Emily Dickinson lived most of her life in seclusion. Her poems were published posthumously and received widespread literary praise for their bold and unconventional style. Her poetic style left a significant legacy on 20th Century poetry.

20. Emmeline Pankhurst 1858-1928
A British suffragette, Emily Pankhurst dedicated her life to the promotion of women's rights. She explored all avenues of protest including violence, public demonstrations, and hunger strikes. She died in 1928, 3 weeks before a law giving all women over 21 the right to vote.

21. Marie Curie 1867-1934
Marie Curie was the first women to receive the Nobel Prize and the first person to win it for 2 separate categories. Her first award was for research into radioactivity (Physics 1903). Her second Nobel prize was for Chemistry in 1911. A few years later she also helped develop the first X-ray machines.

22. Emily Murphy 1868-1933
Emily Murphy was the first women magistrate in the British Empire. In 1927 she joined forces with 4 other Canadian women who sought to challenge an old Canadian law that said, "women should not be counted as persons"

23. Rosa Luxemburg 1870-1919
A leading Marxist revolutionary Rosa Luxemburg was a friend of Lenin who fought passionately to bring Social revolution to Germany. In the lead up to the First World War she wrote fiercely against German imperialism and for international socialism. In 1919, after her attempts to herald a Communist revolution in Germany failed, she was murdered by German soldiers.

24. Helena Rubinstein 1870-1965
Helena Rubinstein formed one of the world's first cosmetic companies. Her business enterprise proved immensely successful and later in life she used her enormous wealth to support charitable enterprises in the fields of education, art, and health.

25. Helen Keller 1880-1968

At the age of 19 months Helen became deaf and blind. Overcoming the frustration of losing both sight and hearing she campaigned tirelessly on behalf of deaf and blind people.

26. Coco Chanel 1883-1971

One of the most innovative fashion designers, Coco Chanel was instrumental in defining feminine style and dress during the 20th Century. Her ideas were revolutionary; in particular she often took traditionally male clothes and redesigned them for the benefit of women. She is listed by TIME magazine as one of the top100 influential people of twentieth Century.

27. Eleanor Roosevelt 1884-1962

Wife and political aide of American president F.D.Roosevelt. In her own right Eleanor made a significant contribution to the field of human rights, a topic she campaigned upon throughout her life. As head of UN human rights commission she helped to draft the 1948 UN declaration of human rights.

28. Amelia Earhart 1897-1937

Amelia Earhart was the first woman to fly across the Atlantic in 1928, just one year after the first ever crossing made by Charles Lindeburg. It was a significant achievement in itself but also significant for being achieved in a male dominated field.

29. Katharine Hepburn 1907-2003

An iconic figure of twentieth Century film Katharine Hepburn won 4 Oscars and received over 12 Oscar nominations. Her lifestyle was unconventional for the time and through her acting and life she helped redefine traditional views of women's role in society.

30. Simone de Beauvoir 1908-1986

One of the leading existentialist philosophers of the twentieth Century Simone de Beauvoir developed a close personal and intellectual relationship with Jean Paul Satre. Simone de Beauvoir radicalised philosophy. In particular, her book "The Second Sex" depicted the traditions of sexism that dominated society and history. The book was received to both intense praise and criticism. It was a defining book for the feminist movement.

31. Mother Teresa 1910-1997

Devoting her life to the service of the poor and dispossessed Mother Teresa became a global icon for selfless service to others. Through her missionary of Charities organisation she personally cared for 1000s of sick and dying people in Calcutta. She was awarded the Nobel Peace prize in 1979.

32. Dorothy Hodgkin 1910-1994

Awarded the Nobel Prize for chemistry, Dorothy Hodgkin worked on critical discoveries of the structure of both penicillin and later insulin. These discoveries led to significant improvements in health care. An outstanding chemist, Dorothy also devoted a large section of her life to the peace movement and promoting nuclear disarmament.

33. Rosa Parks 1913-2005

Rosa Park's refusal to give up her bus seat to a white man indirectly led to some of the most significant civil rights legislation of American history. She sought to play down her role in the civil rights struggle but for her peaceful and dignified campaigning she became one of the most well respected figures in the civil rights movements.

34. Jiang Qing 1914-1991

The wife of Chaiman Mao, Jiang Qing gained tremendous power during the repressions of the Cultural Revolution. Jiang claimed she was only following the orders of Chairman Mao, but in practise she abused her position to pursue political enemies and target anything "intellectual" or "artistic". After the death of Mao, she was tried and convicted.

35. Billie Holiday 1915-1959

Given the title "First Lady of the Blues", Billie Holliday was widely considered to be the greatest and most expressive jazz singer of all time. Her voice was moving in its emotional intensity and poignancy; an intensity probably fuelled by her tempestuous private life. Despite dying at the age of only 44 Billie Holliday helped define the jazz era and her recordings are widely sold today.

36 Indira Gandhi 1917-1984

First female prime minister of India, she was in power from between 1966-77 and 1980-84. Accused of authoritarian tendencies, she only narrowly avoided a military coup by agreeing to hold an election at the end of the "emergency period" of 1977. She was assassinated in 1984 by her Sikh bodyguards. Her murder was in response to her decision to storm the Sikh golden temple, which left many innocent Sikh pilgrims dead.

37. Eva Peron 1919-1952

Eva Peron was widely loved by the ordinary people of Argentina. She campaigned tirelessly for both the poor and for the extension of women's rights. At the same time she was feared by some in power for her popularity. She was also criticised for her intolerance of criticism; with her husband Juan Peron they shut down many independent newspapers. She died aged only 32 in 1952.

38. Betty Frieden 1921-2006

Leading feminist figure of the 1960s. Her book "The Feminine Mystique" became a best seller and received both lavish praise and intense criticism. Betty Frieden campaigned for an extension of female rights and an end to sexual discrimination.

39. Margaret Thatcher 1925 - Present

The first female Prime minister of Great Britain, Mrs Thatcher defined a decade. In particular, she is remembered for her emphasis on individual responsibility and lack of belief in society. She presided over a successful war in the Falklands, reduced the power of trade unions, and her economic policies led to 2 major recessions in the UK.

40. Marilyn Monroe 1926-1962

Born Norma Jean Baker, she rose from childhood poverty to become one of the most iconic film legends. Her films were moderately successful, but her lasting fame came through her photogenic good looks and aura of glamour and sophistication.

41. Anne Frank 1929-1945

Anne Frank's diary is one of the most widely read books in the world. It reveals the thoughts of a young, yet surprisingly mature 13-year-old girl, confined to a secret hiding place. "Despite everything, I believe that people are really good at heart."

42. Audrey Hepburn

Leading female actor of the 1950s and 60s, Audrey Hepburn defined feminine glamour and dignity, and was later voted as most beautiful women of the twentieth century. After her acting career ended in the mid 1960s, she devoted the remaining period of her life to humanitarian work with UNICEF.

43. Dian Fossy 1932-1985

Zoologist and conservationist, Dian Fossey dedicated her life to protecting wild species. In particular she spent most of her life with the wild gorilla in central Africa helping to raise awareness over endangered species.

44. Germaine Greer 1939-Present

Leading feminist icon of the 1960s and 1970s Germaine Greer enjoys raising contentious issues. In particular her book "The Female Eunuch" was a defining manifesto for the feminist movement, which proved influential from the 1960s onwards.

45. Betty Williams 1943-Present

Together with Mairead Corrigan, Betty Williams campaigned passionately to bring an end to the sectarian violence of Northern Ireland. They founded the Community for Peace and were awarded the Nobel Peace Prize in 1977 (post dated for 1976)

46. Betty Jean King 1943-Present

One of the greatest female athletes Billie Jean King was one of the greatest female tennis champions who battled for equal pay for women. She won 67 professional titles including 20 titles at Wimbledon.

47 Benazir Bhutto 1953-Present

Benazir Bhutto was the first female prime minister of a Muslim country. She helped to move Pakistan from a dictatorship to democracy in 1977. She sought to implement social reforms, in particular helping women and the poor. She was forced out of office on corruption charges; charges she continues to deny.

48. Oprah Winfrey 1954-Present

Influential talk show host, Oprah Winfrey was the first women to own her own talk show host. Her show is tremendously influential, usually focusing on issues facing American women.

49 Madonna 1958-Present

Madonna is the most successful female musician of all time. She has sold in excess of 250 million records. In addition to being a great pop musician, she has rarely been out of the limelight.

50. Diana, Princess of Wales 1961-1997

One of the most photographed persons ever, Princess Diana combined the appeal of a Royal princess with her humanitarian charity work. Although her marriage to Prince Charles was overshadowed by affairs on both sides, her popularity remained undimmed as many were inspired by her natural sympathy with the poor and mistreated. Her death in 1997 was a major shock to the whole world and sent the world into an unprecedented collective mourning. many of the Women selected in this list were featured in a book:

"Women Who Changed the World" by Ros Horton and Sally Simmons at Amazon.co.uk

Other Influential Women at Biography Online

- Raisa Gorbachev
- Sung San Suu Kyi
- Julie Andrews
- Hilary Clinton
- Billie Holiday
- Jane Goodall
- Amy Johnson
- Paula Radcliffe
- Odette Sanson
- Tegla Laroupe
- Mary Whitehouse
- Virginia Woolf
- Maya Angelou

Here is one of the most important, but least known women… The higher authorities would prefer her to completely disappear, for her views. Many societies have formed advocating and studying her philosophies.

http://en.wikipedia.org/wiki/Ayn_Rand
http://www.iep.utm.edu/rand/.
www.**aynrand**.org/site/PageServer?...**ayn_rand_aynrand**

The following was taken off the web as well and is well worth reading her story.

Ayn Rand (Ayn rhymes with "mine"), born Alissa (Alice) Zinovievna Rosenbaum (February 2, 1905 - March 6, 1982), was a controversial American philosopher and novelist, most famous for her philosophy of Objectivism. Her philosophy and her fiction both emphasize above all the human individual and the genius of which he is capable. Her novels were based upon the Randian hero, a man whose genius leads others to reject him, but who nonetheless perseveres to prove himself. Rand viewed this hero as the "ideal man" and made it the express goal of her literature to show these men.

Biography Ayn Rand was born to Jewish parents in Saint Petersburg, Russia. She studied philosophy and history at the University of Petrograd. In late 1925 she was granted a visa to visit with American relatives. She arrived in the U.S. in February 1926, at the age of 21. After a brief stay with them in Chicago, she resolved never to return to the USSR and set out for Los Angeles to become a screenwriter. She then changed her name to Ayn Rand, partly to avoid Soviet retaliation against her family for her anti-socialist views.

Initially, Rand struggled in Hollywood and took odd jobs to pay her basic expenses. While working as a Hollywood extra on Cecil B. DeMille's King of Kings she bumped into (on purpose) an aspiring young actor, Frank O'Connor, and married him in 1929.

Her first literary success came with the sale of her screenplay Red Pawn in 1932 to Universal Studios. Rand subsequently wrote the play, The Night of January 16th in 1934 and published two novels, We The Living (1936), and Anthem (1938). Anthem, despite its appearance as a short story, is actually considered by many to be an epic prose poem. We The Living was made into a film six years later, in 1942, by the Italian government under Benito Mussolini, although without Rand's knowledge.

Rand's first major success came with the best-selling novel The Fountainhead (1943). The manuscript for this book was difficult to get into print. It was initially taken from publisher to publisher, collecting rejection slips as it went, before it was picked up by the Bobbs-Merrill Company publishing house. The book was so successful that the royalties and movie rights made Rand famous and financially secure.

In 1947, as a "friendly witness" for the House Committee on Un-American Activities, Rand warned against Communist propagandists in Hollywood. Rand's testimony involved analysis of the 1943 film Song of Russia. Rand testified that the movie grossly misrepresented the socioeconomic conditions in the Soviet Union. She told the committee that the film presented Russia as if it were an amazing paradise of comfort, beauty and plenty for everybody. However, she said, in reality the conditions of the average Russian peasant farmer were appalling. Apparently this 1943 film was intentional wartime propaganda by US patriots. The movie was, at the time, intended to provide comfort to the US public during the American-Soviet alliance during World War II. After the HUAC hearings, when Ayn Rand was asked about her feelings on the effectiveness of their investigations, she described the process as "futile."

Rand's political views were extremely anti-communist, anti-statist, and pro-capitalist. Her writings praised the "heroic" "American values" of egoism and rugged individualism. Her fiction writings often told stories of educated, successful Americans who found their lives unfairly burdened with the hassles of taxation, bureaucracy and other forms of heavy-handed government interference. Rand also had a strong dislike for organized religion and compulsory charity, both of which she believed helped foster a culture of guilt in successful people.

In the early 1950s Rand moved to New York. She gave talks at Yale University, New Haven, Connecticut (1960), Princeton University, New Jersey (1960), Columbia University, New York (1960, 1962), The University of Wisconsin (1961), Johns Hopkins University, Baltimore

(1961), Harvard University, Cambridge (1962), and The Massachusetts Institute of Technology, Cambridge (1962)

In 1951 Rand met the young psychology student Nathaniel Branden, who had read her book The Fountainhead at the age of 14. Branden, now 19, enjoyed discussing Rand's emerging Objectivist philosophy with her. Branden's relationship with Rand eventually took on romantic and sexual aspects, though they were both married at the time. This ultimately ended with the destruction of their partnership, noted later, as well as the failure of an institute begun for the advancement of objectivism.

Rand published the book described as her "magnum opus", Atlas Shrugged in 1957. This book, as with The Fountainhead also became a best seller. According to a joint survey conducted in 1991 by the Library of Congress and the Book of the Month Club, Atlas Shrugged is recognized as the "second most influential book for Americans today", after The Bible by numerous authors. It is also named as one of the "25 books that have most shaped readers lives" in a 1995–1996 list developed with the theme "Shape Your Future—READ!" Atlas Shrugged is most often seen as Rand's most complete statement of Objectivist philosophy in any of her works of fiction. Along with Branden, Rand launched the Objectivist movement to promote her philosophy, which she termed Objectivism.

Throughout the 1960s and 1970s, Rand developed and promoted her Objectivist philosophy through both her fiction and non-fiction works.

Rand's philosophical alliances were few. She acknowledged an intellectual debt to Aristotle and occasionally remarked with approval on specific philosophical positions of e.g. Baruch Spinoza and Thomas Aquinas; she seems also to have respected American rationalist Brand Blanshard. However, she regarded most philosophers (throughout history, not only her contemporaries) as at least incompetent and at most positively evil, singling out Immanuel Kant as the most influential of the latter sort. In general, her treatment of other philosophers is one of the reasons her own nonfiction is sometimes dismissed as pseudophilosophy

Rand broke with both Nathaniel Branden and his wife Barbara Branden in 1968. Ayn Rand described the break to be the result of her finding out about behavior incompatible with the tenets of her Objectivist philosophy.

The Brandens later said that the final break was triggered by Rand finding out about another romantic relationship of Nathaniel Branden.

Ayn Rand died on March 6, 1982 and was interred in the Kensico Cemetery, Valhalla, New York.

Legacy In 1985, Leonard Peikoff, Ayn Rand's designated legal and "intellectual" heir, established the Ayn Rand Institute, the Center for the Advancement of Objectivism. The Institute has since registered the name Ayn Rand as a trademark, despite Ayn Rand's desire that her name never be used to promote the philosophy she developed. During her life Ayn Rand expressed her wishes to keep her name and the philosophy of Objectivism separate. It is understood that this was in order to assure the continued survival of the philosophy she developed once her own life was over.

In 1989, a schism in the movement occurred. Objectivist David Kelley wrote an article called "A Question of Sanction," in which he defended his choice to speak to non-Objectivist libertarian groups. Kelley said that Objectivism was not a "closed system" and condoned tolerance of and intellectual debate with other philosophies. Peikoff, in an article for The Intellectual Activist called "Fact and Value", said that Objectivism is, in fact, closed and that factual truth and moral goodness are intrinsically related. Peikoff essentially expelled Kelley from the Objectivist movement, and Kelley founded The Institute for Objectivist Studies (now known as The Objectivist Center in Poughkeepsie, New York.

Chapter Five: Wealth and Happiness

ANOTHER DELICIOUS MEAL HAS ENDED in the back yard on another beautiful day. Hank no longer able to hold back his burning question blurts out, "Hey Ronny, you've talked about all sorts of subjects so far. We are yearning to hear you're opinion, on wealth and poverty." "I have been waiting for you to ask this question since we started, and I am surprised you held back this long.

"Any way let me read to you an excerpt on something I wrote a little while back." "Sort of like another one of your stories?" Malcolm jokingly interjected. "Yes something like one of my little stories" Ronny answered back with a smile. Reaching under the bar counter Ronny pulled out several sheets of paper and began reading.

Why We Are Always Broke?

One of the major causes of unhappiness is due to money, meaning the lack of it. Money troubles are the root causes of many divorces. This has been a harsh reality lately, due to many layoffs in many areas of business. Usually the main bread winner is affected, causing the bills to mount up. Frustration builds, causing the arguments to become more intense, till finally the inevitable breakup happens.

When children are involved, the situation is then compounded. This results in added monetary strain, child support, lawyer's fees and whatnot.

We end up as a society of broken families. We are not educated on cause and effect in our early years, only to learn the harsh realities the hard way later in life. This information is kept from us by the authorities, for they know that divided we are weak, and that is the way they want it, for we are then easier to control. We are kept ignorant only for this purpose.

There have also been many suicides due to losing major amounts of, or all of one's fortune, also many illnesses have been brought on by stress due to lack of and/or loss of one's earnings, usually through mismanagement or prolonged layoff from one job or a stock market crash. We are ignorant of the fact that it is those at the top of the food chain, those top elite who desire total control, who rule over us.

To subject us to ever increasing debt and deprival, they are the ones who implement the financial disasters we have encountered throughout the decades. If that were not bad enough for the citizens, they will then start some war to further increase our hardships, which in turn helps the chosen top executives to pile even more money into their pockets through military arms production.

We live in a world where it seems that the subject of money, how to earn it, or have it, is the top priority for one's survival and success. We grow up with the thought of the almighty dollar constantly on our minds, how to earn it, how to get it, how to steal it. We buy lottery tickets and go to the casinos with the hopes of winning more, yet 99% of the people never seem to realize that they have lost more then they will ever win, it is all fixed for you to always lose.

In the gambling world, they know that there is a sucker born every minute. It is amazing the number of people who spend all week gambling are constantly losing, and still do not put two and two together. They do not realize that this is an addiction, and is destroying not only their lives but their families as well.

Gone are the days when people traded goods or services for goods or services. At the beginning it was a very simple way to survive, trade for trade. As people gathered together in ever larger groups, such as villages and towns, the barter system began to get ever more complicated.

Until some smart fool decided that sea shells or some type of monetary system was needed to over come these ever evolving problems of simply trading items for services and visa versa. One goat for five chickens or two bales of hay seemed a little difficult. Also chickens and goats were very inconvenient for people to carry in their pockets while traveling.

The invention of money seemed to solve many problems, though unwittingly causing many future ills such as theft and other forms of corruption. The idea of greed for more and more of this labor saving device has ruined many lives ever since. Originally this new found currency was controlled by the ruler of the land, who made the decisions as to its values or its buying power. The populations seemed to accept this new concept since it initially solved some of their problems.

They could now hand some sort of flat disk to another person, and receive a meal, product or service. As time passed, thousands of years later we arrive to the present day. We find ourselves, in a sense, imprisoned by the need of money. It rules our lives in such a complicated manner, this interplay of good and bad intentions. It seems we will never solve this issue of needing or wanting more of these flat disks and pieces of paper with a dollar sign on them.

Our lives are spent in the act of obtaining more and more of this currency that we believe will make our lives so much easier. We trade time for cash, most of us prisoners of the almighty dollar. We spend our time working in factories and offices, digging holes or operating some form of machinery, to make a so called living. We dream of purchasing better things, such as vacations or items for necessity or pleasure. We work for our money and not the other way around, for we have not been trained to do so.

Most people believe that they do not earn enough to get by, but the truth is most really do, it is in the way that the money is handled at the end of the day that places you in a particular bracket of wealth. Often the money drain is out of your control. Why is the expression 'the poor get poorer and the rich get richer?' so common in our world? The answer is very complicated, yet very simple.

There is a mixture of reasons why the poor stay poor. Such as: they buy 'stuff' they do not really need for many reasons, maybe to say to the world we have 'stuff'. Or they are easily conned into that particular purchase, either way that is lost money that could have been used for something useful. Maybe pay off a bill or put a little away into savings. In reality, they mostly squander what little they have, either unknowingly or they have a fear of being in a better place because that involves some kind of extra effort.

Many people in the one hundred thousand dollars a year or less category actually end up living beyond their means, they may have nicer things, but are usually in deeper debt, not much better off than the ones who make twenty thousand dollars a year or less, they just have bigger headaches and more stress. Also, as a result, they seem to work harder as well. In the end, it is all relative to ones earning and spending power. Knowledge of the proper use of ones earnings or lack of knowledge will determine how much one has at the time of retirement.

The act of being frugal is not necessarily being cheap. One can live a nice life while being frugal, and yet enjoy many things in life, even though there might be some small sacrifices here and there from time to time. When one squanders foolishly then the results will be a miserable existence at the end of ones life.

Some examples of being frugal could be, say saving for an item of choice that is worthwhile and actually needed, instead of using the credit card on every purchase. The credit card idea was invented, yes as a convenience in some cases, but mostly to keep many people in debt.

The credit card industry is a business and nothing more. The card allows you the convenience of purchasing an item now, without the need of cold hard cash. You run the risk of late charges via interest for being overdue on just one payment. Therein lies the headache for many people who tend to spend more then they are actually earning per month.

The card is treated as free money by some, while others see it as freedom to purchase that item or service now, not realizing in the moment of purchase that this money must be paid back in the short time span of one month, or service charges will apply in the form of interest.

The credit card companies make themselves look good too, by only asking for a minimum payment. This is a ruse since the minimum payment is only the interest owed, and has nothing to do with the principle part of the bill which is the actual cash you spent. If all you paid was the minimum every month you would never pay it off, never in a million years. The best way out of this is to pay at least two to three times the requested minimum payment per month, or the whole thing in one payment then stay off the card after that.

One main problem here is the high interest rates (legal loan sharking comes to mind). Also the ease of obtaining a card, credit made easy. Most stores and services prefer you to use a credit card. These establishments were sold on the idea of the ease as well, (hey, less cash around preventing the possibility of theft of money left in a safe) used credit card slips are of no value to a thief.

So on it goes, the spiral of debt continues upwards. One very illogical punishment when credit card payments are late is the skilful use of the penalty of higher interest rates, making it more difficult to pay off, not to mention that it will take a lot longer to pay off. Here is where the credit card companies really make a fortune at your expense.

Ways to have your money leave your wallet, paying taxes and there are many kinds of tax, property tax, income tax, tax on purchases. I like this one, death tax, service taxes, gas tax, and the list goes on. Let's not forget service charges, these also are a sort of tax. Advertizing is especially use full in draining more of your hard earned dollars. When you have seen or listened to the advertisements enough times, you will unwittingly buy. This is a great brainwashing gimmick.

Types of expenses such as vehicle breakdown due to poorly designed parts made to wear out. Why is it that cars break down so often? Simple. Since the auto industry makes a fortune on after market repairs and replacement parts. It's all designed to break down or rust, so that you have to buy a new one. They think that is the best way to keep them selves in business.

Here is a thought. Do you think they would have to be competing with imports if they had built better, more efficient products? Do you think there might have been less layoffs in the auto industry if the cars, trucks, and vans had been built of better quality? Do you think we would have bought more North American autos?

The other thing is, say, an auto manufacturer is producing three different cars, and here is the kicker, they all have the same chassis, same basic body styles and interiors, but they put extra chrome on some and/or gadgets in another. And charge three different prices for basically the same car. Now, they all rust at the same time, they all have the same type of break downs, worn out parts, and yet have different costs. This does not make sense to me.

The same goes for almost every other product. Products are designed to be used two or three times then thrown away, hence the throw away society, with more garbage taken to the dumps. That's a lot of money being buried and made into a big hill to play or golf on when it is full. Then it's off to the next location to dump even more wasted money. Do you see any logic here?

Then there is the extended warranty insurance they con you into buying with your product, say a fridge, stove, washer, dryer, TV system, or car. Why don't they just tell you the thing is going to break down in an estimated amount of time. Usually the part that does break down is very cheap and easy to fix, but you have paid about four times what it was worth in warranty payments. Well, if it makes you feel better having the ease of mind, then buy the warranty (insurance).

The replacing of other mechanical devices is another money drain. Fast ageing items such as household items. The expression "you get what you pay for" applies. Then unnecessarily buying, of overly advertised products and services to, obtain money from you, brainwashing you into believing that you must have or need this item or service.

This item is old (but still useful) get rid of it, and get this shiny new one at twice the cost of the old one. Keep up with the Jones's show your newly purchased item to your friends and family who then feel the need to go out and get one, so as not to feel left out or deprived.

Agencies that cost: The present society that we are in has grown and evolved into such a large and complicated system. That it has made it very easy for many agencies to practically fleece the majority of the public. Lawyers are making a killing because of so many laws and regulations that the bulk of the populations is rarely aware of until it is too late. Court cases are on the rise, with no sign of slowing down.

The number of people, as well as companies that are being sued every year continues to rise, causing more money to flow into the pockets of the legal beagles, or should I say, down the drain. Here is mostly where evil people cause many innocent and honest, hard- working individuals and companies needless stress and financial loss. Even jail terms are not unheard of, where many honest innocent people suffer this injustice.

Interest rates are designed to keep you in debt as long as possible, including high interest rates. Interest rates for bank loans, interest rates for mortgages, credit card interest, interest rates on government loans to foreign interests. That is what you are really paying for, and you did not even okay that one, did you?

We can not forget the churches, now can we? For this would be blasphemy. We are conned into giving to our churches which do not pay taxes. Yet most of the older churches are built of better quality materials than our own homes are, and we only visit them on Sundays while the rest of the time we live in run down shacks in comparison.

Living our lives around the decisions based on the ideas of others, be it governments religions, businesses, services such as utilities, doctors, lawyers, etc. You are led to believe that you are not capable of being empowered or allowed to use your own mind in making decisions.

Life insurance is another money drain which I cannot really argue over but, it is the type of life insurance that is the problem. Whole life with dividends is the worst of the two evils here. Term life would be better for a young family especially if there is only one bread winner, then, it should only be enough to pay the funeral costs and all other bills, with a little extra to help the family manage for at least a year. Some insurance will help with funeral costs, but those that do not really need it are wasting their money.

There is no proper training in school to prepare you in the managing of your money once you enter the working world. In fact, very few ever get the proper training from any one. The chosen few are the lucky ones who are able to prosper better then most. Did you know that it is your government that has failed you, and has done so on purpose, starting not too long after the signing of 'Declaration of Independence.'?

That is, most of those at the very top, who hold the power for prestige and glory for themselves only. Sadly only a rare few, who were there in positions of power, were there with honest intent. Politicians of ill repute started butchering the Declaration of Independence in the USA, as well as the Constitution in Canada for their own greed, slowly hacking away at the freedoms of the citizens. Through the ensuing years the people began losing more and more of their rights and freedoms.

Picture yourself accompanying a friend or relative to the hospital, for some medical tests, which will take several hours, which no doubt most of us have done. Have you ever walked around, or gone to the cafeteria for a coffee or a snack? I would expect that ninety nine percent of you did not think too much about what you might have been observing, apart from looking at the clock and wondering how much longer you would be waiting for your friend or relative to be finished with the tests.

A very small percentage would have been observing all sorts of things, such as the amount of actual patients versus hospital staff, versus just the people there to accompany friends or relatives. We all know that every person sees with differing view points. So here is one example of a persons view of what he sees and what is going through his mind, as he sits there drinking a coffee and eating a cinnamon twist.

Well the coffee was made with chlorinated water which actually damages brain cells and causes other medical problems. While the coffee grounds have added ingredients to want you to go back for more. The cinnamon twist was made with white flour, and is covered with icing containing too much of a chemically produced sugar.

He realizes that every one else is basically eating and drinking the same unhealthy foods and beverages, and the sad thing here is that they are all blissfully unaware that these product have been instrumental in getting them to be in this hospital in the first place.

He is sadly aware that all of the people coming and going, walking here and there, many in wheelchairs too obese to walk. While others, are in wheelchairs due to some chemically caused disease, or an actual accident. They all have no idea of the sinister forces that have caused them to be at this place at this time.

The amount of money being spent (wasted) is staggering. The fuel burnt to get here. The earnings lost, parking fees, staff salaries, hospital equipment, heating costs, electrical costs, medical supplies for tests and operations, and the list goes on.

The observer feels as if he were an alien visiting a surreal, illogical world, where self- induced illnesses and diseases is the normal way of life. As if to live to kill one self were normal. Not to mention the wasting of resources and time in a place called a hospital.

Do not be confused by the previous statements. Actually hospitals are very handy to have, especially if you are involved in some sort of accident.

In reality the hospital is unknowingly causing its own problems, such as the wasteful use of supplies and equipment. An example would be, buying new office equipment, for the doctors and staff lounges, while the housekeeping staff must deal with only one, thirty year old machine to clean mops, rags, lifters, restraints, curtains, and such. No, the doctor's charges have not been forgotten as more expenses.

Their need to hand out prescription after prescription helps them make more money, which is okay for them, but not for you. You are the one paying outrageous prices for drugs that cost pennies to produce, worst of all these drugs with all the side effects cause even more health problems. It is a vicious circle for you to pay and pay for drugs that send you further down the road to bad health.

Did you ever stop to consider, say one example for where your money goes? We will say this example is a search for a cure for Diabetes. When was it decided that we should start to have people contribute hard earned money for this cause? Let us assume that we started fifty years ago 1959.

First ask yourself the question: After fifty years and still the cure has not been found? Why? Are the many thousands of doctors and research scientists with fifty years of ongoing research really that ignorant? Or are they being suppressed in giving out positive information on found cures?

If so by whom? Who would stand to lose mega dollars if the truth about a cure for Diabetes were found? Well that one is easy to answer, and that is the pharmaceutical companies and organizations whose lively hood depends on donations from the public that is kept in the dark. Let us be very conservative and say that only $20,000,000 dollars is raised every year for fifty years

$20,000,000.00 x 50 = $1,000,000,000.00 dollars One billion dollars

This is only one fund raiser for one medical problem. If you were to add all the fund raisers for all the medical problems, the amount of money raised, or should I say slyly taken from your wallets, is staggering. This is done through the use of sympathy, pleading for you to help others with medical problems.

The ploy here is to make you feel guilty to be the healthy one. What if you needed the cure one day, won't you feel foolish for being so cheap to give so little to help so much? As mentioned earlier, this is one more way to drain your wallet of money that could be better used somewhere else.

Any person who looks at this very conservative number and, that does not include the rest of the world where the amount would be in the billions and trillions donated to research, and yet a cure has not been found? Something is definitely wrong here. For you it is another money grab from your wallet, not to mention your health. You are being conned into donating for any type of medical cause.

Rest assured that any money you donate to any type of medical research will never, ever result in a cure. These dishonest organizations con millions of people worldwide to volunteer their own time and money, to collect from more innocent people to give up their hard earned money. The money collected goes into special accounts where it is then divided up to the assorted agencies who then grease their wallets, little actually goes to research. Then if any cure is found it is kept hidden.

Hank stood up and began clapping as Ronny finished reading, followed by the rest, still astonished by what they had just heard. Richie and his wife Alice stood up and approached Ronny who by now had his arm wrapped around Catherine. "Ronny," Alice declared "Richie has something to say." Richie positioned himself on the deck in such a way so that all could see and hear him.

"Alice and I want to thank Ronny and Catherine for being such great friends.

We think, and I am sure you will all agree, that so far we have learned more and grown mentally and spiritually in the past few weeks then ever in our lives. We feel privileged and honored being your friends. Alice and I want to publicly thank you for this privilege. Thank you, Ronny and Catherine from the bottom of our hearts." The rest all stood up and clapped in approval. James yelled out. "Let's have a drink to celebrate"

Ronny, visibly shaken, smiled then grabbed Richie's hand in a warm shake. "You have not even heard me talk to you on some little tricks that you could use to get yourselves out of the ruts you now find yourselves." All were grateful to hear that more positive information was to come.

"Okay everyone, sit down. You my also want to take notes" Ronny paused for a moment while they searched for pens and pads to write on. Hank did not need to be asked, for he was always taking notes. "Has any one heard the expression 'If you can't afford it you don't need it?'" The odd yes was heard from the group.

"Well my father used to tell me that if you don't have the cash to purchase something that you think you want, or ask yourself, do I really need it? Will it make my life better, or will I be happier with this item? You will discover that most often it really will not improve anything by purchasing whatever it is you think you want at the time.

"Do you know what happens here?" Ronny asked the group. A moment of silence, followed by 'I don't knows' from those seated. Ronny pressed on "you just saved yourself some money. Now let's look at this another way. Say instead of paying by debit/cash, you used a credit card, because there was not enough money in your wallet or bank account.

"Here is what will happen. By using your credit card you have now placed yourself behind the eight ball. In other words you are now in debt, that's not saving. That's losing through future interest payments. The only real winner here is the credit card company.

"Now, if you had saved up for that item, you would have paid cash with no future interest payments, and you are not in debt. See the difference?" hmm's and hah's could be heard at this time. "Also, by the time you saved up for that item, there is a good possibility that you find that you really did not need it. If you still found yourself wanting it, there is also the possibility that the price came down and you are able to pay less than if you purchased it in the first place." "Good point," someone said.

"The younger you are the easier it can be if you plan on being a millionaire by the time you are sixty-five, even if you work for someone else. Here is how. Have payroll or the bank automatically take out of your cheque that is every time you are paid. Two, three, five, ten or more percent of your gross pay. Choose the percentage you feel most comfortable with in the beginning then up it when, and if, you can.

"They then put that money into a savings account for you, hopefully one that pays a decent interest rate. Soon you will not notice that little bit of money not being there in your cheque. You will be surprised that you can live without it. Note, it is very important that you don't touch it under any circumstances, for it is your future well being we are talking about here.

"Along with this plan, stay as far away from using a credit card as possible. Pay cash as much as you can for everything. Save up for something, do without now to enjoy later when you're retired. Now I'm not saying to starve yourself or wear rags, but be frugal. Remember your early vacations are paid for with the vacation pay you receive from your place of employment.

"Plan your future by putting money aside for that. It is a shame that so many people do not do these simple things, then, end up living in poverty in retirement. It is like the story of the grasshopper and the ant. Some people retire well off and well fed while others are poor and hungry.

It will be better eating hamburgers vs. cat food, right?" That was fully agreed upon by the group.

"Purchase mid range quality items. Stop trying to keep up with the Jones's, walk when you can, reuse, recycle. Do whatever it takes to save. You can do all this and still be happy and live decently. If something works stay with it. Ask yourself, do I really need the next fad? Will my world end if I don't have it?

"There were no planes, cars, TV's, or computers a little over a hundred years ago. Yet people still got around, read the news papers, and lived good quality lives.

"For more detailed information on what I just covered, I strongly urge you to read the book (Automatic Millionaire) by David Bach I understand that it is available at some banks for free. In Canada it is available at the Scotia bank. Also David Bach is on the New York Times best selling of (Start Late, Finish Rich) and

(Smart Women Finish Rich)."

Chapter Six: Some thoughts on History

JEFF ASKED IF RONNY HAD any opinion on history. Ronny promptly replied "yes I do, but first I'll give you my opinion on war."

Take note of a minor detail that is rarely if ever mentioned in the history of war. Never once is a politician or owner of a production company fabricating items of war ever actually involved on the battle field during a battle. Only the lowest level of the population is used as cannon fodder. They are disposable items of war, for the glory of the upper levels of society.

Innocent souls are sent to the front line to do the bidding of the rulers of the time. Why, then, do we die for some politician who in the end, really does not value our lives? Upon returning home the vets are given some small, cheap token of appreciation for their valor. Most vets spend the rest of their lives mistreated by the politicians or most disgustingly, forgotten for their heroism and valor. Many die lonely and destitute.

The only real reason there is a person called a soldier is for doing the bidding of some ruler or politician. It is when the politician is not happy with the answer of some other bureaucrat, they get angry with each other and send their forces to attack the other to settle political or religious disputes.

All the while, some greedy business person is making vast sums of money for the productions of war materials. Are we gullible enough to think the leaders don't get a kick back here as well? The reality is that war, for some, is very profitable.

There have been many instances where the civilian is asked to donate materials to the war effort. Do you think they are compensated for this? The answer is 'ABSOLUTLY NOT'. Yet when all this material arrives at the factory it is turned into items of war, whose only purpose is mutilation, destruction, and death. Yes, when the items are produced they are sold at a profit. As for those that donated, well maybe they will get a thank you.

Here are some examples; WWI Germany, church bells were expropriated from many towns and villages. The brass was turned into shell casings for cannons and guns. Lead water pipes were ripped out of the ground to make bullets. WWII North America, nylons, pots, pans, iron railings, tin cans, and old tires, to name a few. These things were turned into war planes, tanks, ships, parachutes, and many other items of war. Bottom line, free scrap to make a profit and someone dies.

Why should we fight their stupid battles? We should let them settle their own stupid disputes by themselves. Let them have, say a hundred acres to play the game of death, but leave the rest of the world at peace and untouched by the curse of war. We will leave someone on the outside to make sure they do no stray while we stay alive and healthy and productive.

Why is it that so many people say it will never change in our lifetimes? It is they who have given up the fight, they feel defeated, that you, cannot fight the system. Yes, you can fight the system, but you must do it right.

Years ago I saw many pictures and movies especially of the Viet Nam war. What I saw were to me atrocities and felt so ashamed to be a human being. In those days I did not quite comprehend why these horrible events should happen to people. When a country is invaded and its people try to defend themselves, they are considered the enemy.

These supposedly evil people are only trying to defend their own land, are murdered then often decapitated, and their heads are held up, proudly shown off as trophies, much like the killing of a wild animal. Meanwhile all the poor soul whose body is now in pieces was just defending himself, his family, and country from the aggressors.

The Hitler's and Stalin's have caused the deaths of millions, many their own country men. People of value, those with the ability to think and produce great works of art or business, philosophers, were brutally sent away to concentrations camps most never to be seen again. People who spoke out or had a different point of view, were suspect of some imagined crime and were never seen again. Not to mention the pain of loneliness and loss of the loved ones left behind.

A great source of cheap labor indeed, they were fed very little and forced to work to death. No pity, no remorse, no proper funeral, just placed in a pile and cremated, or thrown into mass graves. It would, of course, be right to think that if these horrors only had happened in the twentieth century, people would have been appalled, and the major part of the population would have objected and done something about it. The problem with man's mindset is that we have lived with this 'life is cheap' for thousands of years attitude and we can't do a thing about it.

It is mind boggling that man can perform horrible harm and death upon fellow man. This type of mind must be an evil in itself, incapable of sympathy or guilt, some form of deformity of the mind and/or soul. One with the ability to slash, mutilate, and kill. Then walk away to clean the knife or rifle, sit down and have something to eat, all the while joking and bragging.

It beats plowing a field right? Well, idiot, who will plow the fields after you've killed them all off? Who will plant your crops, build your houses, make your cars, and make your clothes? Did you ever think about that Mr. Evil person?

In the twentieth century, from, 1900 to 1999, the worst possible century of man in terms of murder and abuse, yet so far up to this point in time, the greatest in advancements of technology. Hundreds of millions of human beings were murdered to satisfy the wishes of a few evil sub-humans who somehow achieved the power over the masses. A huge dishonesty to humanity indeed perpetrated through lies and deceit. Those in power who have attained absolute power have all each caused the death of millions.

Yet there is still a small group of power mad individuals out there that want absolute power. We shall not let them have it. When and if we ask who placed these dictators in power, why should we be surprised to find out that we are the ones that put them there? They used lies and deceit to achieve these positions of power.

At the beginning of the twentieth century the world had its first major world conflict. 'The war to end all wars the biggest joke on humanity in history'. This war was one of the ugliest ever seen. Men lived in the trenches filled with mud, excrement and death everywhere for long periods of time. The soldiers were then sent over the top into the meat grinder, suffering death and all sorts of mutilations at the sound of a whistle, something akin to animals at a slaughter house.

All the while, the generals sat comfortably very far away drinking tea with crumpets. Wondering how the battle was progressing, they sat and waited for results. This was the way it was for both sides of the trenches. One tends to think that before this particular conflict, some very high ups decided that the world needed a reduction in the population, so it was decided to plan this exercise of death.

Sure, great advancements were made in the field of medicines, especially plastic surgery, but at what cost to human suffering? Also new forms of illnesses were introduced such as shell shock, from the constant bombing of cannons far off in the distance. This trauma effected men in ways never seen before.

The tragedy here is most were made a fool of and told to get back in the trenches, thus proving, to any thinking person, that all these poor souls, were just cannon fodder. A life to sacrifice to the God's of war. The authorities even found ways to reduce, and often times eliminate the pay such as the pensions of many of the mentally wounded.

Many nations had volunteers to go to battle. These men had no idea of what they would see or endure, and some deserted. Those that deserted were then captured, and placed before a firing squad to be shot to death. The question here is, why punish a volunteer? The higher ranking officers answer, to make sure the rest stay in line.

Today, almost a hundred years later, human body parts and unexploded bombs are still being found on these old battle fields of needless death. What good did it all do for the progress of humanity? It did very little since only a chosen few became very wealthy selling arms and politicians remained alive and unharmed. In the end it sowed the seeds for a next world war, causing again more pain and suffering and death, along with unbelievable collateral damage.

World War II took place in many more countries then World War I. Consequently, there were many more people killed and much, much more collateral damage as many more cities town and villages were involved. Many millions of civilian deaths were caused by bombing of cities, basically flattening whole sections that, at one time, supported life and productivity.

The worst blight, of course, were mass killings in an attempt at exterminating certain peoples. This was called 'the cleansing' by the Nazis. The Russians basically did the same thing to millions of others, their way of getting rid of undesirables. These types of heartless acts are continued up to this day by other countries. Some are not as well known about due to media blackouts.

Through out history, young men, fathers, brothers, and uncles have gone to war, for the glory of God and country. There are a number of reasons, either to defend or invade while pillaging and plundering. Most often spurred on by valor glory and adventure. What glory is there in death and mutilation? Where is the glory in killing a fellow human? Where is the good in ransacking, burning and destroying life and property?

With all the men who went to war, how many returned home happy and fulfilled, satisfied with a job well done? Feeling no remorse with what they did, saw, or suffered? Very few do. Talk to and observe veterans who visit war cemeteries. They all leave with tear filled eyes, having lost friends, close buddies, and wonder how and why they themselves survived.

The expression 'War is Hell' could not be better said and is so true. Most veterans never get past that. It is always with them, this never ending nightmare. Yet many are proud or at least put up the front of being proud, possibly to hide the fact from everyone else that they served. They defended their country from the so called oppressors of freedom. To this day, most war monuments are cared for by civilians rather then government agencies.

Not too many realize that many regular soldiers in the so called enemy side have been brainwashed with the same idea's, that they too are defending their freedom and country.

Veterans from both sides were used as cannon fodder for the glory of some politician or tyrant. Nor did they realize they were victims of brainwashing of whatever country. Some now realize this, most do not. One day man will learn to say 'NO' and tell the leaders to fight their own battles.

Jeff finally interrupted saying "Wow stop there. That's quite a mouthful. You seem to be very agitated as you speak about all this Ronny." "Yes I get very emotional when talking, even thinking about this type of subject. Because it is all interrelated with everything else we are discussing. What I am saying is that we live in a world of what many people that I am associated with would say is an upside down world, illogical and backwards in its thinking.

"In my mind, man's inhumanity to man started many thousands of years ago. Some warlord from some strange and far off place came charging into some little hamlet or village, killing and plundering. Leaving its people dead and the town in flames, for what reason, I ask? Was it because they looked different, or spoke a different language? Perhaps, they had some valuables, or were a perceived threat, to the invading horde. Events such as these perpetuated revenge.

"As we travel through time, we come upon many such events that changed history. A major one would be the Spanish discovering what we now call the America's. This event was a great blessing to the Europeans at the time, but was devastating to the native peoples on both the Southern and Northern Continents; what we now call North America and South America.

"In those early times, the Spanish did not explore peacefully to build trade agreements with the native inhabitants. As soon as they understood that there was much gold to be plundered, that is all they saw. They did not see human lives or any other wonders. So many lives and much knowledge forever lost, in both Americas. Lives lost through killings and spread through diseases that the natives had no way of dealing with. Lost knowledge through thoughtless ransacking and destroying what was not understood or considered ungodly.

"In the USA, the people celebrate Columbus Day. The American First Nation people do not celebrate this day from what I understand. I do not blame them either, for they have lost it all. Their heritage, language, and most of all their lands and way of life were brutally taken from them.

"Treaties were signed then broken, by the white man many times. Most often these treaties were nothing more then a con job to allow the white man to gain a section of land that had some form of value, such as gold, silver or some other commodity which the natives, at the time, had no use for or did not comprehend.

"And if that were not bad enough they were insulted by being placed on Reservations, and told not to stray, virtual prisoners in their own lands, Lands that were loved and taken care of for countless generations. They saw their lands plowed under, mined, and opened up in a variety of desecrations. Then they were treated as second or third class citizens when they volunteered for war."

Malcolm stood up saying, "I have noticed a gradual change in the mindset of the film makers over the years. The old western movies portrayed the Indians as mindless savages. Massacres were the Indians fault and only they did that sort of thing. That the white man was always the innocent victim, that the cowboys always won the battles because the white man was good and the Indians were evil savages.

"Now a day's, the film makers seem to be more honest in their attempt to be historically correct in representing both sides of the story. In my mind" continued Malcolm, "The movie 'Little Big Man' with Dustin Hoffman was the first time we could see the story from both sides. We see in this movie a more honest version of events then from years before."

Ronny then asked the group. "Of all man's inventions, which one item was, or is, at this time the most mass produced? I'm talking about inventions throughout history. For this should give you food for thought. If you boil it right down and think very hard you will come up with some very interesting answers or possibilities. How about arrows? Since the invention of the bow there has to have been millions of arrows made, right? What about swords?"

Martin stepped in and said "what about coffee cups, since millions of people drink several cups of coffee every day." "That's a good one," Ronny returned. "But has anyone considered the bullet starting with the invention of the gun which includes hand guns, rifles, machine guns, and the Gatling gun. Everyone knows what the arrow, spear, sword, and bullet are used for right?"

"To kill or maim," came the unanimous reply. "Correct." answered Ronny. "Maybe now you might have a better understanding of how I feel and think in regards to an authority that uses force and intimidation on its own people, who in turn, are sent to use force and most often deadly force against other Nations.

"This as I have already told you has been going on for thousands of years. Yet I believe that one day, when enough people on this planet wake up and become enlightened, lasting peace, happiness and prosperity for all will be achieved. It is our birthright.

"I was born and raised Roman Catholic, and by the age of twelve I realized that there was too much hypocrisy in the church and so much death was caused by religions. Those are the reasons why I have the attitude I now have towards religions. They place us in boxes and teach us that we are different from others. We are segregated in race, creed, and color.

"But we are all one family' even though we do not look the same. We all bleed red blood. A black man's blood can save a white, yellow or red man's life. These so called authorities, be it religion or governments, have caused us to be separated from each other. They taught us to hate and not trust each other. Yet we have seen, in many instances, where people of various races and creeds have worked and suffered together for a common goal."

Martin asked "What can I do what can anybody do?" Then continued with "how can one individual change the world?" Ronny answered "Do what I am doing, the same thing that Jesus, Buddha, and Mohammad did, they preached then got others to do the same. The only difference here is subject matter.

"I am not trying to form a new religion. I am only trying to inform you of some of the things that I think are wrong in this world. There are better, more educated, and informed people than me out there doing what I am doing here now. This way we use what has been termed the 'multiplier effect'.

"Here is an example; Catherine and I are telling you as a group. Then all of you start your own groups, and so on and so on. I am sure you all understand." They all agreed. Ronny continued "Talk to people, write a book or short story. Get others to tell others and others to write more books. I don't like the word, but make it a cause, a crusade if you will.

"The more people that become aware and enlightened, the easier and sooner the chains will fall. The sooner we will gain the freedom we lost twenty three hundred years ago. The sooner the misery and suffering of third world countries as well as those in poverty in our own country, will end.

"Say no to the warlords, put down the rifles and the bombs. Turn the tanks back into plows. End the destruction and begin the construction of life, liberty, and happiness for all. I mean the whole planet, not just the fortunate rich countries. Make love and compassion a way of life for every single human being on this planet.

"All this begins here now with me and you. I am not alone this concept started a long time ago. Many people throughout the ages have voiced it, lived it. Today it is spreading at an ever faster rate. It is not happening like 2,3,4,5 but 2,4,8,16,32. Within a very short time from now we will hit what is known as the tipping point.

"At that time, the progress will increase exponentially. We are on the cusp of the next great revolutionary leap for mankind. It is a new movement, a new way of thinking, finding out about ourselves. We are creators of our own lives, our own destiny. We are learning that we have the power within ourselves to create the life we desire.

"We do not, and have never needed, an outside authority to tell us what to do, what we need or want. We can do say and think for ourselves. The sooner you, as an individual, realize that you are you own authority, the sooner you will be free. This freedom will affect several more, which will then each affect several more, and so on, and so on.

"The more that know, then the more that talk and enlighten others. Thus the 'ripple effect' continues and grows. Till eventually the whole planet is affected, resulting in a freedom that the world has not seen for over two thousand, three hundred years."

Chapter Seven:
Possible Better Future World

"You keep talking about how bad everything has been throughout history, on how we are being controlled and abused. What are your views on making things better?" inquired Shelly. Richie and Alice both agreed. "Yes we would also like to know" Ronny who had been cleaning the BBQ, turned to Catherine asking her to finish cleaning the grill, then turned towards Shelly and began talking.

"To get an idea of what life would be like in a new world without war and the way we perceive of the present governing system, we would have to change into a totally different system, such as a protection only government protecting its citizens.

"Meaning all national armies stay within their own borders, (unless at the requested of another country on a temporary basis for defense only). With all other sections of government just simply disbanded, with all assets sold to pay off any debt. Taxes would be reduced significantly, health care would be easier to achieve, foods would be healthier.

"The cost of gas, and electricity would be greatly reduced, alternate sources of power would be allowed to develop and distributed without the intervention of the cartels, which at present have government backing to protect them. The cost of food and shelter would also drop. No person on this planet would go hungry, or uneducated, all would live with dignity.

"Picture a world with clean air, beautiful cities, no crime to speak of, no wars, or borders. A world where you can travel to work or go on vacation anywhere you choose, in comfort and style. To get a further idea of what such a world would look like, check out the "Venus Project" developed by a genius of a man called Jacque Fresco, from Florida. Listen to him speak, look at his ideas, you will be amazed. In such a world we could all live a happy, healthy, prosperous, life.

"Unfortunately there will no doubt be some casualties on account of ignorance and fear of changing the status quo. Some of those in power at this time will not relinquish their positions easily, thereby causing harm and/or death to some innocent individuals. There are always those that do not want, or fear change. They will do what it takes to keep things the way they are. They cannot conceive anything better, or fear of losing their comfort zone.

"This new government should be run by business minded people with no political career aspirations or hidden agendas. This way they can be fired on the spot from the office they are running, if it is discovered that they are only there to benefit themselves. Also, they would not have the power to use force or coercion to enforce any of their own ideas. It is my opinion that a properly run business is more efficient and cost effective then any government run system.

"So many people are at present hard at work with their own theories of a better way of life, without taxes or war. Some groups are working on ways of changing the face and workings of our government as we see it today. The intended changes are to be done peacefully; no coups or civil war is intended or wanted.

Life is far too valuable to be wasted or destroyed.

"Here is where we have to disband any, and all, of the government policies. Locate and disband the groups who actually believe in killing individuals who are for the people. So many assassinations have been committed by groups who fear or do not wan, positive change. It is imperative that these groups cease to exist in a world of real and true freedom.

"Imagine a government that is truly and honestly for the people by the people. With no hidden agendas, hiding nothing, and demanding nothing, only true protection. Eventually, with an honest change in government, all ideas of a better life could blend into an almost perfect way of life. We must make sure though that our eventual way of life is not etched in stone, for we must always evolve and learn. If we stop evolving and learning we will stagnate and die.

"It is man's nature to constantly seek answers, new and better ways of doing things, to produce and create. This way we are able to evolve to higher levels of the mind. It is not the final destination, but the actual trip that is important to us.

"These things may seem impossible to achieve, according to some who believe that you can not change the present system. Yes, the system can and must be changed, and yes, you can do it by talking to your friends, relatives, and neighbors. Spread the word and eventually there will be enough people to make it all happen.

"Of course all of this will not come about easily. There will be many who will be against it, some will not want to give up positions of power and prestige, other for fear of something new and different, afraid of change. Others will not like it for they will no longer be spoon fed by the system, not realizing the system would eventually enslave them.

"Many in the top leadership positions would fight very hard to keep their way of life, which is to control and tax us. They will use any means possible to keep things from changing. The only real backing they will have are those too lazy to do anything for themselves, those that depend on the system.

"This, of course, will require a drastic change in the human psyche, changing from a rotten system to one of honest integration, something that should have happened two thousand, three hundred years ago. For we have been deceived and controlled for the last 2300 years, by politics and religions, all because of a man called Plato.

"Plato's ideas and philosophies were adapted by those seeking power and control, from his time up to now. Plato was, in reality, a traitor to freedoms and rights of man. Plato's ideology was chosen over a true hero, Aristotle whose philosophies were based on individuality and freedom.

"Plato preached slavery, and sacrifice of one's individuality to serve and die for a leader, selflessness, team player, one's life meant nothing to the state. Because of him, democracy is another form of slavery. From here at the time of Plato begins the 2300 years of deception against humanity. Aristotle preached free thinking, productivity, individual oneness, honesty.

"Jesus himself was a free thinker. He was a conscious individual. He realized that many people in his time were not aware. They listened to the voices in their heads or to the voice of an external authority. In a word they were bicameral, meaning they had no concept of yesterday and tomorrow, of deception and guilt, a caveman mentality, yet having speech and a sophisticated language.

"In other words Jesus became, or was conscious. He realized right from wrong, past, present, and future. Good and bad. He did not listen to the voice in his head, he was aware that it was him thinking, not the voice of authority, while the bicameral mind listened and obeyed.

"He understood that those who were unaware (bicameral) just needed to hear things differently than from what they were brought up with. These people who would hear things said in a different way could then be awakened to a level of consciousness as we know today.

"Jesus was only trying to explain these concepts in the only way they could comprehend. That is in what we would today define as parables. The leaders of the time who themselves were conscious were afraid of losing the power and control over the masses. They had to somehow stop Jesus from preaching.

"The leaders were aware of Plato's philosophies and had adopted them for their own ends. This system was working well till this upstart know it all called Jesus entered the picture. Jesus started telling the uneducated people the truth. Something had to be done and quickly, and so Jesus was crucified.

"To understand the concept of the bicameral mind in more detail, I suggest you read the book by Julian Jaynes. 'The Bicameral Mind' The origin of consciousness in the break down of the bicameral mind. Or if you go on the web and search for Julian Jaynes, there you will gain a better understanding of this bicameral concept.

"From the time of Plato, religions and governments adopted his teachings which exist to this day. The Catholic Religion which was founded around 250 AD adopted these Platonist ideas, which then turned civilization in Europe backwards into the dark ages, thus perpetuating the 2300 year deception.

"The church became so powerful in those early times, that it actually influenced, and at times controlled, the governments and Kingdoms of many European countries throughout the ages. As time passed, its control widened to other countries, due to the quest for power and control over the masses. Much valuable information and knowledge was either destroyed or hidden from the public.

"In those early centuries, the church thereby held complete control by keeping the people ignorant. The church, at that time, was so intent on keeping control it started the crusades, which lasted many years resulting in thousands upon thousands of needless deaths.

"Secret societies upon secret societies formed, and exist to this day, controlling much of what goes on in this world. For the sake of humanities proper evolution, this control must end. We never really needed, nor wanted, to be ruled by a few individuals.

"It is time for the ideologies of Aristotle to now be adapted, and get rid of the Platonist rule which humanity has been a victim of for the last twenty three hundred years. Throughout history right up to this very day, religions and governments (and in the old days, kingdoms) were and still are based on Plato's ideas and philosophies.

"We the citizens of Earth must take our freedom back, simply by saying 'No' to the authorities. An authority who rules by force and intimidation, taxing us to death and treating us as cannon fodder, and or sheep with no minds of our own. Civil war is not being condoned here, nor is any kind of violence intended or cited. Martin Luther King had the right idea, Freedom and Independence through education and non-violence just as Gandhi and many others have taught.

"Nor is turning the other cheek intended, defense where defense is needed. The cheek has been turned for the last 2300 years. It is time to adopt Aristotle's views and ideologies world wide. It is time for the world to be run by integrated honesty, for the betterment of the Earth and all life dwelling upon it. If not, we will surely destroy it.

"Greed and dishonest power have existed for far too long, causing pain, death and destruction, only to appease those in power, holding humanity from our rightful destiny of value creation and beauty, wealth, health, and happiness.

"Throughout history we have been segregated to form separate and distinct countries and differing cultures. These distinctions were used as an easy way to produce conflicts, rather then free trades and the sharing of resources. We lived with the idea of taking by force what we wanted. This ended up destroying many natural resources along with causing much death and misery.

"Hate and prejudice must fade away and replaced by honest love, understanding and kindness, allowing the free flow of valuable information, and ideas to be shared equally. Knowledge must be available to every individual on Earth, along with health, wealth, and happiness. It is our right to have the freedom to choose to do and think in any way that is productive to ones self and others.

"Do not be deceived when you are told that there is not enough for all. The planet's resources cannot support its present and future populations. This is due to so much mismanagement of resources by careless individuals and bumbling bureaucracy. Profit is usually a contributing factor here.

"There is enough for all, let it be shared and used by all. The benefits to the world would be mind boggling. Who knows what good will be created and achieved in a free independent world of value creators giving us health, wealth, and happiness?"

"That is all very interesting" Jeff said, "Do you have any stories to go along with all this?" Ronny pulled several sheets of paper from his back pocket. As he unfolded the pages he announced, "I wrote this several months ago, shall I read it to you?" "yes." replied the group in unison. "Thought you would never ask" Ronny said grinning.

Way Out:

So ask your selves, who is going to save us from this coming world of imprisonment and slavery that those in power are planning so diligently to bring about? Well the answer is very simple, although it will be very difficult to bring about. It is you, me, and many other people who are fed up with the present system, who have the faith and inclination to rock the boat and sink it. What is the boat? 'Burden on Advancing Technology'. We must sink it to build our own.

We hear about 2012 as the end of things, the world as we know it will change, for better or worse we do not know. Most religions fear this coming event, prophesies from many sources. Even the governments have some fear as well. One wonders maybe it is the end of all religious and evil governmental powers, and a new world of personal freedoms that they see on the horizon.

Why, then, are we shown only destruction and death, the end of life? Total destruction, complete nothing. Is it their fear of lost power and control? They would not be able to survive in this new world of freedoms and bounty, because they have not contributed anything of value. They would starve and wither away to nothing. They have spent their lives only taking.

We, on the other hand, have been working and producing values for ourselves and the rest of the world. We will survive and prosper in full honesty and will make a better world for ourselves. A world without force or intimidation will be ours. Free to think and grow, healthy and prosperous. We will be free to achieve great heights, to advance human knowledge, without infringements from some higher authority.

There will, of course, be growing pains in between the change over to this new world of peace and prosperity. We, as humans, have this insatiable appetite to solve problems to explore new worlds. The world of fantasy will become the world of reality. In other words the world we live in today can be called 'The A/C World' meaning 'Against Civilization' an upside down version of what should be, but is not.

We will create the 'C of U' meaning "Civilization of Universal possibilities". We will live in a world where technologies will advance at ever faster rates (without government burdens that stagnate, growth and vision). Advancements in medicines will be staggering, once freed from the strangle hold of the greedy bureaucracies.

There are many groups and societies out there trying to inform and enlighten as many people as they can, to the harsh realities of lies and deceit of our governing systems, medical, and food industries keep hidden from us. It is a long and difficult task especially when the majority is either too closed minded or brainwashed by a corrupt news delivery and advertizing system.

These systems are owned and operated by those in power be it government with medical, and food manufactures payoffs. In effect, legal bribes by the larger manufactures with government backing are forcing new enterprises and entrepreneurs many needless difficulties in starting out, causing most new startups to fail, especially if these new enterprises show promise to be beneficial to the general public.

It is mind boggling to note that many are not aware of how much has been lost and stolen from us, by corrupt agencies, manufactures and individuals so that can keep their positions of power and influence. The list of benefits lost is long, here are some examples.

A deliciously, healthy, bread was removed from the market because the bread, was healthy. A carburetor that could get over one hundred miles per gallon was never mass produced why, because you would save money on gas. The cures for many diseases are not made public why, because you would be healthy and not need as many drugs. These are just a few examples.

These many groups and societies are only trying to enlighten the public as to how they can be free of this ruling curse. What life would be like under self rule and decision making, showing them the unbounded prosperity, health, and happiness that would result with the vanquishing of the corrupt systems that, at present rule over us like demigods. The resulting effects would be drastic improvements in all aspects of our lives, once we are out of the control of useless, crippling rules and regulations.

Most of these rules and regulations are placed there for no other reason but to delay and provide extra cost to the public. The more ways that government can come up with to take money from us, the weaker in their eyes we become. So getting rid of constricting rules and regulations would stimulate fantastic advances in all technologies. Thus making life easier for us all, we would be wealthier from lowered costs, and healthier from better foods.

Fortunately the number of open minded individuals seeking truth and knowledge is growing steadily, helping to spread the truth to others willing to listen and learn. Our main objective, at this point, is to reach the tipping point, before we are all locked into a life of misery and servitude. Most importantly our main objective is getting past the nuclear threshold, before some extremist idiot presses the button of nuclear inhalation. This is one threat we must not fail to eliminate.

Lucky for us there is a group out there under the guidance of a highly intelligent integrated thinker, who has formed the bases of a political party, political in terms of the present thinking of the majority of society at this time. This man has discovered and mapped ways to cover the loopholes caused by dishonest politicians to the Declaration of Independence.

He presents a political party with no hidden agendas, to free the people, so that all may live in wealth, health, and dignity including the poor. His vision of the world is that of prosperity, happiness, and long life. Please note that his ideas are not far fetched and out of this world.

Many people have already benefited and are positively affected by his teachings and guidance. They are living happy, prosperous, enlightened lives. I know this, since I and Catherine are two of these people. And the numbers are steadily growing.

Either way, a world of death and destruction vs. a world of imprisonment and slavery should not be the ultimate end of the thinking conscious human race. We have the right to progress to far greater heights of achievement, with the freedom of our thoughts and ideas. Not to be a slave to some subhuman's idea of glory.

Possibilities to imagine:

Is it possible to imagine a world where - children do not grow up with a hearing impediment because one of Hitler's buzz bombs landed too close and blew out tiny ear drums?

Is it possible to imagine a world where - children can run around and play without the fear of being blown to smithereens from some forgotten land mine?

Is it possible to imagine a world where - a child or a parent or a spouse, does not think daily of a loved one lost and/or killed in battle?

Is it possible to imagine a world where – health, wealth, and happiness is common place?

Is it possible to imagine a world where – all disease is wiped out?

Is it possible to imagine a world where – you can buy food that is healthy and full of nutrition?

Is it possible to imagine a world where – even though you are not a millionaire you have the buying power of one?

Is it possible to imagine a world where – poverty and death do not exist?

Is it possible to imagine a world where – there is no property taxes, almost all other taxes to be non-existent as well?

Is it possible to imagine a world where - war does not happen? No need of soldiers going off to war?

Is it possible to imagine a world where – every one receives a proper education in order to fulfill their desires and be a productive and happy citizen?

Just some questions to ask yourselves, mostly to realize that these are not pipe dreams. Many enlightened people are trying very hard to change this world. Their work is very difficult because of the present system, whose only job it is to keep all of the above questions unanswered, or they would lose their positions of power. Yet, one by one, we are building in number, soon through persistence dedication and the enlightening of friends and family, we will attain the tipping point to bring about the necessary changes for the betterment of mankind.

We also know that many will be kicking and fighting to prevent such a change for fear of something new. The question is 'Do we change for the better? Or do we blow ourselves up?' I would sooner change for the good, since I have grown fond of the idea of living a long and happy life.

"You just keep coming up with stuff to make us think" commented Hank, as he closed his notebook and placing his pen in his shirt pocket. "I hope that I am not boring all of you," Ronny responded as he returned the pages to his back pocket.

Jeff leaned over to Jen and whispered in her ear saying "Am I ever glad we are here listening to all this." Jen nodded and answered. "I never knew of any of this stuff and I agree. I'm glad were here too."

Chapter Eight: Energy Cartels

"By the way, what do you know about energy?" as Hank recovered his pen from his shirt pocket and opened up his note book. Catherine suggested that Ronny talk about the energy cartels such as oil and electricity, to which Ronny agreed.

"In Australia, a man was able to convert an internal combustion gas engine to run strictly on water. He drove it for several months performing assorted tests on it. He was then approached by several men representing the oil cartel who allowed him to test it. Several months later he was found dead, having fallen off the back of a train while apparently drunk.

"This incident seems very strange, since his friends knew him to be a non-drinker. I find it very odd that someone would do something so out of the ordinary and end up dead, when they have everything to live for. Especially something that would make him extremely wealthy and benefit mankind.

"It is a well known fact that the oil cartels want total monopoly over this type of energy. The world moves on oil and oil products. Fossil fuels are limited and they know it, but will do everything in their power to keep the planet dependent on it. Even to the point of squashing any new technology that would end their control. When will short minded, greedy, inconsiderate individuals stop? So many great ideas have been lost to the general population, ideas that would have benefited the world and make it a totally different place then it is today.

"Why should top executives in the oil and gas companies be paid salaries close to a million and sometimes more per year? They, most often, receive large bonuses as well. As has been said before, it's all about the money. As usual it is the consumer that foots the bill. One must ask what type of work, do these people do to earn such large salaries.

"Those that control the energies, such as oil and electricity want total control, this way they have the power to keep us where we are, virtual prisoners to their distorted visions of what the world should be. As many famous people have already said 'It's all about the money'. 'To hell with the planet and its resources, they are mine, all mine, and I will not share'. First of all they are not yours, who in their right mind ever said they were yours? I surely did not give them to you so that you could cheat the rest of humanity, and keep them prisoner to your greed.

"Many garage entrepreneurs and inventors have, and will continue to, come up with ground breaking inventions. Innocently they show the various energy cartels these ideas in the hopes of making some fortune. Some do, by receiving a small payoff, while others simply, vanish, as if they never existed. If the world only knew how many lives have been lost and/or destroyed, (which is still happening to this day) to keep the energy cartels in power. Hopefully one day the truth will be known.

"The auto industry is also standing along side as well. Why was Henry Ford allowed to build and grow? Well, simply because he was an originator of the assembly line and a very important asset to the oil and other energy cartels at the time. Anyway there was really no other automotive competition then. But after that, any upstart company had to fight tooth and nail, and many perished. Why? Well, since the energy and automotive cartels were so powerful they virtually control the government, who will side with them, making it extremely difficult for new businesses to start.

"Tucker, an up and coming auto manufacturer, was forced out of business by the big three with the help of the government. Tucker had introduced many innovative ideas; these greatly concerned the big three.

They feared lost revenue and control over what the public was, in a sense, forced to buy.

"Not only Tucker, who was in the auto industry, but many others in different industries were financially and physically destroyed by the evil and greedy. Anyone who came up with an idea or product which could have been beneficial, in any way, to society was silenced in whatever way possible. Sort of like a murder made to look like a suicide. Keep in mind here that anyone who had a product or an idea that could harm, or was absolutely useless to health or happiness, was allowed to continue.

"Why do you think the government is always bailing out these huge companies, who claim to make huge profits in quarterly reports, and yet always seem to need to be bailed out for any number of reasons? These large profits are going into the coffers of many greedy individuals, and also for legal payoffs.

"By the way if you or I tried to do this, we would be accused of bribery and arrested. So if you are in bed with the government on these levels its legal, hmm, sort of a double standard here. If these businesses were properly and most importantly HONESTLY operated there would be no need for government intervention or assistance.

"To show how improper it all is, the governments, who, in turn, hide the facts by attempting to show the public that they are placing controls and regulations on these cartels, when, in fact, all these controls and regulations are just a ruse. They have no teeth, just a paint job, to make the public think that they have some sort of protection. One wonders where the real power is, the government or the cartels? If you have, or will, invent, a revolutionary energy saving device, be very wary of your health and life.

"It is my opinion that the government should keep its nose out of the day to day operation of any business, large or small. If a business succeeds, it does so on its own merit, likewise if it fails, it fails. The government's only real reason for being is for the protection of the people, and only that. Nothing more. Unfortunately, it has evolved into the mammoth, blood sucking monster it is today. With so many different departments, each with their own agendas, controlling our lives in every which way possible.

'We the majority, have lived under the influence of those in power for far too long. With very little chance of making changes of our own to better ourselves and the rest of mankind.

"As time passes, large companies grow ever larger and more influential and powerful. Now, I am not against a company for making a profit and growing, but what is wrong with the system of having extra large corporations is that they tend to destroy or make it extremely difficult for smaller startup businesses to gain a niche in the market. This, to me, is not honest business practice.

"What is meant by this are two things:

1. The smaller business has a difficult time growing and maturing, to create a healthy and competitive livelihood.
2. The purchasing public is not allowed to choose where and who to buy from.

"When, there is a variety of choices in business locations for the consumer there is less chance for us to be stuck in a monopoly. Monopolies should be banned.

"Anyone remembering the cold war against Communist Russia might recall scenes of how bare the stores were in most cities in Russia. As you enter the store, here is what you would see. One size and brand of, lets say beans, or one kind of bread, also the shelves were never full, containing one or two boxes or cans here and there. These stores were nowhere near to containing the volume or variety we find in North America.

"The point here is, yes we have a variety of foods (the quality is questionable) and other products. It is our energies, such as only oil, gas, diesel, and propane (all non renewable) and hydro or atomic electricity (little wind, solar, or other) that we can be allowed to produce ourselves.

"There are many other forms of energy, that we, the majority, do not have a chance to purchase, because of the existing cartels control their release or research and development. There is a very high possibility the new forms do exist, and when all the oil reserves are used up, then they will be introduced. You guessed it, we will have no choice but to purchase only from the existing cartels.

This, in itself, is a form of world domination.

Jeff and Jen stood up at the same instant and started asking the same question independent of each other. Once realizing this, they stopped and looked at each other and started to laugh, causing everyone else to start laughing as well. Finally Jeff said as he pointed to Jen, "ladies first." Jen therefore asked the question they both had started. "Ronny can you give us some idea of what you mean on each of the cartels? I mean what are some of the ways that they are, oh I don't know, like gauging us?"

Ronny replied "Gladly. Let us start with Oil. Have you ever given it any thought as to why the price for a barrel of oil is always going up?" "The workers on the rigs want to be paid more," someone shouted. Catherine interjected by saying, "the workers are well paid, and there are not enough of them to make a dent in the system even if they all demanded an instant raise."

Ronny continued, "Partially. it is because the oil barons want to make as much of a profit as possible, and will continuously raise prices till someone says that's high enough or the majority of the public is unable to afford such high prices. The oil barons know that one day the fossil fuels will run out, so it is in their best interest to get while the getting is good.

"The oil refining companies who buy the crude oil also make a huge profit. They are then able to pay many CEO's and other top executives millions of dollars per year. Yet many top government leaders don't get anywhere near that type of salary. We, the consumer never know from one day to the next what the price of gas will be. Just like a yoyo up and down, constantly never knowing when will it stop?

"The prices are up slightly in the morning then lower late at night, then back up the following morning. Oh, let's not forget the day of the week makes a difference also. Then we have a long weekend. Watch the prices skyrocket. Also some gas stations charge more then others, what is the reasoning here? Oh, yes because they claim their gas is better, since it contains special additives and cleaners.

"Where, in reality, this makes little difference in performance and gas mileage, but some people are gullible. If you do not see this and realize that they have you in their back pocket, then you must be blind.

"The auto and oil industries are so closely linked that they are almost Siamese twins, both dependent on the others survival. This produces a very large and powerful cartel, thereby making it practically impossible to introduce a new form of energy. Car manufactures claim to be working on alternate sources of power, but are very slow to produce anything. Yet new sources have been available for generations, but were banned or hidden from the public. Hey that's one way of sucking every possible penny from an old technology before introducing a new one.

"If you were to look back at the automotive industry, you would find that there were many, fine advancements that could have made a difference today. Sadly these bright achievements were discarded for mere profit, instead of our comfort and safety, let alone the atmosphere and the world's fossil fuels. Many innovative ideas were bought then shelved, or destroyed because they would save on fuel or were an alternate form of fuel. Some examples would be the carburetor that could give you one hundred or more miles to the gallon of gas. The other was a water fuel, or hydrogen fuel.

"The electric car was introduced in the nineteen twenties but did not last long. It was taken off the market with the excuse of being to expense to produce or some thing or other. I believe it is because if more were produced it would have put a serious dent in the oil profits.

"Just think about this; after ninety years of refinements, the electric car would be very efficient today. Also, oil and gas prices would be nowhere near as high as they are today. The constant up and down fluctuations would possibly not be happening as they do these days.

"Instead, they introduce a fuel injection system that, from what I understand purposefully wastes a small percentage of fuel as well. The catalytic converteris another waste of fuel.

"The Electrical companies have many ways as well to inflict higher and higher prices on the consumer. What, the river running over the dam decided to raise its price for flowing through the tunnels, past the turbines producing electricity? The atom said 'we will not atomize any more' till you pay us a higher amount, and threaten to shut down the atomic energy? I don't think so.

"The workers want a raise, so the company exports that cost to the consumer. The electrical companies send out X amount of kilowatts per day and expect to be paid for said amount. Now we all know that the hydro wires are not perfectly insulated. For example when you are near a high power line you can almost hear it sing. You are warned to stay away from these wires, or you will be electrocuted.

"The electrical companies tell you that you are paying for a form of grey energy waste, where your appliances are stealing power even when they are shut off. That's a form of extra charge to you. You are also paying for lost power from the external lines, before that power even reaches your meter, lost power in the form of shorts, here and there which drain power from the lines, sometimes into the ground or into the atmosphere.

"You are charged higher rates if you live in rural areas since there are longer runs of wire going to you, verses living in a high density area where meters are closer to each other. My question is why we should have to pay for lost hydro, due to inadequate insulation of the wires?

"We, in, Ontario, Canada, are paying down a 32 Billion dollar debt that was caused by Ontario Hydro many years ago. This debt should finally be paid off around 2012, if we're lucky. There are, in my mind several questions here. First off, why should the public be forced to pay for a debt they did not cause? Second, where did most of the thirty-two billion dollars go?

"Many people are aware that quite a few top executives received very large bonuses, some in the millions of dollars, prior to Ontario Hydro going under, to be taken over by Hydro One. If there had been any honesty here between the old hydro company and the government at the time, this debt would not have existed, let alone forcing the public to pay it off.

"It is not like this is the first time this type of thing has happened. It appears to be an ongoing thing all over. People in high positions are getting much greedier and skimming off the top. This, however, tends to cause higher and higher prices, with a rise in inflation. The worst thing is, they get away with down right theft, because of their positions.

"The auto industry did nothing to prevent what we call today 'the throw away society', by building vehicles that they decided we needed rather then what we wanted, likewise building autos that lasted for a few short years before they were just scrap, to be thrown away so that we would purchase a new one. Whole industries were based on the recycling of the auto industry, making it cheaper to use recycled metals, yet prices kept going up.

"We have lived in a time of greed for thousands of years. However, since the beginning of the industrial revolution that greed has multiplied. Manufactures are producing items that are easily mass produced, and used for a short time, only to be thrown away with out much thought for recycling. To say nothing of the waste generated by mobile phones, millions are discarded daily. Plastic drinking bottles with a one time use is again highly wasteful. These are just two items, and you know yourself that there are many more.

"Because of the throwaway mentality for the way products are produced we find our landscape littered with garbage. Not to mention the amount of landfill sites required and filled to capacity. We find ourselves constantly needing more and more sites to dump our garbage. Much of it is packaging materials that contained products that will also find their way to the dumps.

"Much of this garbage is produced by people whose only interest is profit with no care or concern for the environment. Most of the waste, if properly thought out with integrated honesty and concern for the environment, could be eliminated. Millions of dollars could be saved by cutting down of waste processing plants and dumpsite fees.

"The governments, in their wisdom, have decided that the best way to beat this problem is to charge us dumping fees for batteries, phones, computers, tires and other items not covered by regular garbage disposal methods. I ask you, how stupid is this, to charge us for some greedy idiot's misuse of resources? They must be paying the politicians off in some way that they will call legalized bribery.

When will they enforce the producers into making something recyclable, or better still, make it to last for years?

"We the general public, must, through force and intimidation, pay for the stupidity of others, who produce the short lasting products. Also the bureaucratic idiots who make up these stupid and useless laws, and for some unknown reason fail to enforce stiffer regulations regarding product life, along with packaging."

Ronny stopped there saying "there is much more to say on this subject but the hour is late. We will discus it in more detail at some future date." They all agreed to meet the following weekend then headed home.

Chapter Nine:
Sign Posts of 2012

"Ronny, what is your opinion of 2012?" Inquired Hank. Ronny responded. "In the Christian faith, I am not sure if other religions have the same or similar belief, my thought is this. In the Christian faith the belief is that when the second coming of Christ happens, there will be something called a rapture when all the believers will rise again and all those still living will disappear from view. Then you will see things like the four horsemen and the breaking of the seven seals and whatnot.

"There will be terrible wars along with natural upheavals. Basically, a purification of the rest of humanity, and finally Christ will appear again and bring peace. That will be the beginning of the golden age on Earth. This is but one of the many prophecies that we have received over the centuries.

"The 2012 prophecies made by the Inca Calendar, Nostradamus, Edgar Casey, and many others, predict a major event of some kind. Some believe in the possibly of a major shifting of the tectonic plates which would change the balance of the planet, resulting in the shifting of the North and South poles. A meteor could hit the planet causing massive exterminations.

"Many fear it will be disastrous, like the end of all life, major wars, horrible storms and earthquakes, while others believe it will be the beginning of a new golden age of man. Wealth health and prosperity will abound, no more poverty anywhere on the planet. All humans will live in wealth and happiness.

"Have you noticed the amount of disaster-type movies produced in recent years? Movies that show humanity in ruins, world societies destroyed. According to the movie makers, we really have quite the choice for our destruction.

"Let's see. We have tectonic shifting causing massive earthquakes, volcanic activity, and large sections of land sinking under the waves. Then there are super volcanoes, that envelope the world in lava and ash fallout. We have whole continents sinking under the seas turning our planet into a water world. Then also global destruction through nuclear wars. Lets not forget alien invasions destroying all life on the planet. Last of all we have some super virus killing over ninety percent of the human race.

"Maybe some new form of government would enter the picture where existing governments lose their power over the people, where the people actually have a say, and control. This would, of course, come from a new political party that has no career politicians. They would implement a prime law policy advocating no force, coercion, or intimidation.

"This new party would be run by business minded people whose sole purpose would be to reduce or eliminate taxes by forceful means, to free up garage entrepreneurs, while disbanding many needless sections of the present governing system. This would, of course, release the financial drain on the budgets.

"Military spending would be drastically reduced. The poor would live healthier, wealthier, happier, lives. Prices would drop while the quality goes up. Needless laws and regulations would disappear. Most everyone would be employed in one form or another. In other words our lifestyles would dramatically improve.

"There would be less need for hospitals and health clinics (as well as health insurance) since most diseases would be eradicated within a few short years. We would live longer healthier lives. The idea of a new political party being elected then changing things for the better, making the people happy, and wealthier is probably the biggest danger for the present political parties.

"Now don't get me wrong here. I am just trying to point out a similarity of what I have been learning and observing. That is, something is coming and it is beautiful. The world is on the verge of a change. In other words, the world as we know it today will drastically change for the better. Like a golden age of peace and harmony. Whether it is from planetary alignment, some solar winds, or some flare from the center of our galaxy causing some sort of DNA change within all of us, filtering out those with evil hearts is not certain.

"This change within us will bring us closer to our true selves, in closer contact with the universe, our true home. We will attain a clearer understanding of our true oneness. That is one step closer, to perfection, is humanities next major evolutionary step. We will have the ability to reach for the stars with just the mere whim of thought. This is all just hypothetical of course.

"Those that are searching and learning about our true selves will be at the front showing the way for others. The love that we have growing inside each of us is very special. As we learn to love, and spread this love around to all others, we are then able to realize our true selves. We will then be masters of all that we create, without limit.

"Maybe I should rephrase that, we all have love within us. That is our power, our energy, our life force. We already have all the love that there is within us. We just need to remember that we are love; we have love, we just need to use it more honestly and openly.

"2012 seems to be a point in time, which we as humans existing in this physical form, with the limited mental understanding of what is out there. Our capabilities yet unknown to us which I keep hearing is what we all have in one form or another. Apparently we all have our own unique abilities and gifts, which we will discover and utilize at some future date.

"We will be able to manifest our thoughts for the betterment of ourselves, and those around us, almost like shopping at the general store of the universe. Our imaginations will determine the power levels of our thoughts. From a simple item to highly complex items will be ours to imagine and receive, from the very small to galaxy sizes, or larger. The beauty that we will be able to create will be astonishing. We will be the ultimate creators. Age and death will be non-existent, meaningless for we will have the ability to vanquish these diseases.

"I can not believe that the prophecies will lead us to some sort of extinction or of the1984 idea that Big Brother is watching you, or that we will be prisoners of some sort of world power. For we, as the human race, have suffered enough throughout the ages.

"There is a group of people who feel that they are the true masters of this world. They are at the top of the pyramid, that those below them are nothing more then mindless servants to be used as they see fit. Through some idiotic mindset, it is felt that close to ninety percent (90%) of the present world population should be culled (exterminated, destroyed, killed). For in their minds, these self imposed owners of the planet feel that all others apart from them are consuming valuable nonrenewable food resources; that ninety percent of people are useless food eaters and should be disposed of like garbage.

"If there is a shortage of resources it is because there is such a unwarranted waste and needless destruction of what we have. The idea of ownership is the biggest negative, the biggest lie, and the cause of much hardship throughout time. If you got to it first, it was yours and most often would not share, and if you did there was a price to pay. This is cruel, unjust, and extremely childish and immature.

"Yet we, because of our long standing mindset accept this, and pay for something that someone else has found. He did not produce it or buy it from someone else. We in our arrogance, throughout history, have done this. Now, if he found it and did something with it, then of course he should be paid.

"A perfect example of this is when Columbus first set foot in the New World (This includes North and South America) He proclaimed that all lands from where he stood belonged to Spain. It did not occur to

Columbus that this would have a huge impact on the natives who were here first.

"With all of the many individuals who have become enlightened and have been teaching others, this information of the freedom of the mind has been spreading for generations now, like an under current, like a loud and beautiful cheer of glorious freedom, ready to break free from the shackles, this prison of hate and desperation. The veil of darkness and despair is starting to rip and slide away from the happiness and joy that is truly and rightfully ours, to have and to hold without fear or intimidation. Allowing us to finally become the value creators we were always meant to be.

"We have to believe that there are more good people on the planet then there are bad ones. We are nearing the end of time, where a few bad people rule over and control the masses of good and honest people. It has been said that recently there are more enlightened people then ever before. Here to help bring about the new age, the Glorious Golden age.

"We will enter an age of prosperity and peace, which is our birthright. Our minds and our technologies have evolved to this point, to bring about our destiny. Some say it has been foretold and many want it to happen, yet there are some in positions of power who fear it, and therefore spread the word of doom.

"These people who fear, these prophesies, unfortunately are in positions of power and thus control the media. They in turn use it to spread fear, gloom and doom for all of us. We must not fall for this lie, this trap of ignorance and fear.

"Let us not continue this trend of submission to an authority whose only purpose is the continuation of its selfish survival. We live under an authority sustaining itself by continuously overtaxing and burdening its citizens with useless time and money wasting laws and regulations. Life is complicated enough without having to add to it with idiotic rules.

"The Inca calendar stops at a specific date in 2012, but does not give any more detail, or it has been purposely hidden from us. Many more prophets throughout the centuries have mentioned this date as well, and again few details are available as to the final results.

"We must always believe in the positive, or there is no good reason to be alive. Since when is it such a sin to want happiness for ourselves, and our fellow man? When one's thoughts are negative, negative things happen. When there are more positive minds thinking positive, loving thoughts, the odds are better to ensure positive results, like a positive brighter future.

"Then there is always the possibility that 2012 will be just another year and not much could happen. Something like the scare of the Y2K bug that was supposed to cause all of the computers to crash, like some big time syntax error. We all found out that on Jan 1st 2000 when our computers continued to function like they were built to do. So let's be positive and think good happy thoughts.

"Let me throw this thought at you. Had the idea of implementing the ideologies of Plato not happened. The results of our present system would not exist. The governments at the time would not have been as warlike. Jesus himself would not have been crucified, giving birth to the Catholic Religion 250 years later.

"Say per chance, that at the time of Aristotle, his philosophies had been accepted world wide, where the individual is most important. That the idea of servitude and self sacrifice for king and country were not necessary. Can you imagine, that from Aristotle's time to say 250 AD the amount of lives that would have been saved. These lives would have produced many great and wonderful things. History would be so different, instead of death and destruction there would have been productive growth and prosperity.

"Now we are at 250 AD when the Catholic religion was formally organized. Two possibilities could have happened here. Possibility number one; would be that this scourge never came about, to enslave all those unfortunate to belong to it/or to be killed by its dogmas, while causing the suffering and abuses in its wake. Possibility number two is that it did form and became one of the biggest blessings on humanity.

"Because of the pure love that it could have taught, this would not have resulted in lost knowledge, and wars against other religions, such as the Muslim religion. If both could have co-existed side by side, sharing dogmas and knowledge. Imagine the amount of lives that would have been sparred, resulting in ever larger amounts of gained knowledge.

"The technologies we enjoy today could have existed , say in the year 610 AD or 810 AD. Then just think of where we would be 2010. Yes I know that I just mentioned is just speculation , fanciful imagination. The point I am trying to make here is that dishonest, evil hearted men in the past stole all that from us.

"They did it to achieve their own personal greedy ends, then taught succeeding generations to continue deceiving their fellow human beings. The results of all this are a history of war, deaths, control, and lost knowledge, producing so much hatred that abounds on this planet.

"I, ask you, who in their right mind would want this system to continue for the next two thousand years? So if your like me, and are fed up with being used and abused, tell as many friends and relatives that will listen. Let them know that great and wonderful changes are just over the horizon.

"All we need to do is act. When a new political party appears promising great things for the public, listen to them, check out their bylaws, and mission statements. Look at their visions and imagine these visions as a reality, because without you, change will not happen. Yes, you can make a difference, by talking to as many as you can, and most importantly, to vote for something new.

Chapter Ten:
Epilogue

THE SUMMER FLOWED INTO FALL then into winter, and still the group meetings continued, till finally they formed their own groups, forwarding the knowledge they had learned to still more people. Those in the surrounding back yards filled the gaps left by the ones that left. Still, the original group stayed in touch with Ronny and Catherine.

Eventually most of the subdivision was thirsting for this new found information, till it became clear to Ronny and Catherine that their home was too small. They eventually had to find ever larger spaces to give their seminars. Eventually they were invited to speaking engagements all over the country, spreading their words of enlightenment to anyone who would listen.

Through all of this, they became famous and very much wealthier. The new found income allowed them the means to form schools for teaching others, to spread the word and make a good living at it.

A year and a half had passed since the first backyard BBQ. Martin and Shelly organized a get together of the original group for the sole purpose of tracking the progress, and staying in touch with their friends. The appointed day had arrived and everyone was in attendance, much to the joy of Martin and Shelly for they knew of the busy schedules that some of them had. Martin and Shelly were grateful that all made it a point to be there.

"We, all know how Ronny and Catherine are doing," announced Martin as he began his meeting. "We are all grateful for their words of wisdom and friendship." With this the group applauded and yelled praises of gratitude, to which Ronny and Catherine shyly accepted. "We only wanted to help our friends, and we had no idea that it would go this far," said Catherine.

"Well, we are all better off because you did. You have not only helped us to a better understanding. Because of you both, thousands more have been enlightened, and the numbers grow daily. You and Ronny started this" Martin replied. "Now let's hear how the rest of the group has grown. Let's start with Malcolm and Grace."

As Malcolm and Grace walked to the front of the room, there was much hooting and hollering with wows and haws and wolf type whistling. Malcolm and Grace had lost their excess weight and were now looking like the perfect couple. They were joined by their son and daughter who were now, also, very fit looking and healthy.

Malcolm began "Grace, the children, and I would like to thank you Ronny and Catherine, for your love, understanding, and guidance. Because of you two Grace and I are in perfect health. Our family is now eating the proper foods and we are all physically active. We lead a healthier, happier, richer life that has enabled us to start our own business."

Grace continued, "when people come to our office, the first thing they see is our before and after pictures, and you know how I hated my picture taken. Now I am proud of it. Those people that see these before and after pictures of our family are then able to truly believe the same thing can happen to them. In most instances, it does.

"We travel all over the country doing seminars, we even sell do-it-yourself DVD's with a one hundred percent guarantee. We have never received a notice for a refund, because the instructions are fun and it's easy to follow the diet and exercise." "Well done," Catherine said as she gave them a hug. Martin came up to congratulate them then said "let's hear from Hank now."

As Hank approached the front, they noticed him with a new woman. "Well it seems that some of us benefited very well from what we learned over the year. I myself took notes and from these was able to write a book, which I might add is doing very well. I am now financially stable and have learned how to save and invest my money. Because of that, I have met this beautiful woman you see standing beside me. Her name is Linda and we are engaged to be married next year. The group applauded then congratulated Hank and introduced themselves to his lady friend Linda.

Next came James: "As you all know I've gone into the field of natural medicines. I will be graduating in a few years. I want to thank Ronny and Catherine for showing me that this type of medical knowledge actually existed. I have already been able to help many people. Several have even helped finance my studies.

"My family is now is now living healthier. Oh, yes. Once I graduate I want to open a clinic, then help other graduates to open their own so that we can spread the idea of natural medicines to ever larger areas of the population."

Jeff and Jen bubbling with exuberance rushed to the front of the room. The rest of the group could not help but notice the unbridled love in each other's eyes, and Jen's face was radiant as she was expecting their first child. They had married four months after the first BBQ at Ronnie's place.

Jeff, beaming with pride spoke, "Jen and I have learned and grown so much. This has helped us to love and care for each other in ways that we never dreamed of. Because of Ronny and all of you we now have a wonderful future ahead of us. We have a lot to teach our children.

"We also started a small business in teaching how to deal with your parents; parents and children can attend together. We have already noticed less violence in our own neighborhood. Our office walls are plastered with thank you letters from both parents and kids. We are even thinking of expanding. After this success, we've also developed another course on living with your Life Mate." Jeff turned to Catherine who nodded her head in approval.

Richie and Alice were up next, Alice started first which shocked the group for she had always been very silent and shy. Now she was more relaxed and self-assured. "I am so proud of my Richie for what he is now doing by studying to be a lawyer. You know we joined the same society that Ronny and Catherine are a part of. Together Richie and I have read and studied the books we received.

"Through them we learned so much more. These books taught us to become more integrated and knowledgeable. We now understand where our problems originated from, and have been able to deal with them. The more we read the more we understood.

"Therefore, I can support my Richie as he studies to be a lawyer. So that he can help many innocent people from the oppressive government system, defended by greedy and dishonest lawyers. He will use integrated honesty as he defends his clients, by using the system against itself. In this, he has already started by advising some good lawyers who then have won their own cases.

"They have told him that when he has passed the bar exams that he will run their office, since they are now reading the same books we have they will call their office 'True Justice with Integrated Honesty'" Richie concluded. "We already have several lawyers and one judge who are afraid to face us in court." This caused the group to burst out in laughter.

Ronny stepped to the front announcing "I am so proud of all of you for having accomplished what you have so far. But we have not heard from Martin and Shelly yet. We should at this time thank them for organizing this get together, then introduce them to tell us how they are doing. So come up here Martin and Shelly." Ronny stepped back as they took his place.

Martin started by saying, "Thank you Ronny and Catherine." Shelly grabbed Martin's hand then spoke "I too thank the two of you, for you have helped Martin and me out of our shells. We are now more self assured and have control of our lives Martin has learned to manifest his desires. The confusion we had at the beginning of all this has completely vanished.

"Martin started a construction business and it is doing well. I help console troubled church goers at the church we attend. Even though we are not the avid members we once were, I do it more to help ease confusion that many people still have.

"No the story does not end here but will continue till the world has changed for the betterment of all. This is like the stone thrown into the pond with only the first few ripples visible. They the ripples will grow wider (as more and more people become aware) the ripples will also grow ever wider. Soon the water in the pond will be totally covered with ripples as will the whole planet will be aware.

"These ripples represent the knowledge which will bring peace, health, wealth and happiness to the whole planet. When all the inhabitants of the planet are released from the fog of ignorance and the Platonic authority, we will then be truly free. All will vanish and be forgotten like a bad dream, where we will awaken to a bright beautiful new dawn.

"Our new day, will guided by Aristotle's foundation of individuality and freedom to choose, awakening new found creative thinking, freeing all of mankind to the joys of happy productive lives. Those that choose not to pass this information onwards only delay the day of freedom. Only by becoming the neighborhood voice can change be made. Those that choose to be silent not only imprison themselves, but their fellow man as well.

"I am not particularly fond of clichés but here goes. 'Divided we are weak, united we are strong.'

References

http://www.youtube.com/watch?v=nKsgOyO5Ntw&NR=1

http://www.stockpilefood.com/

http://www.davidickebooks.co.uk/index.php

http://media.ktradionetwork.com/media/images/coldwell/coldwell.html

http://www.ktradionetwork.com/

http://www.youtube.com/watch?v=c6SqHXrNE-0

http://www.globalhealthfreedom.org/

http://www.youtube.com/watch?v=_gWmVtn5JsA